# EXTREME
# RUNNING

# EXTREME
# RUNNING

## Kym McConnell & Dave Horsley
### WITH FOREWORD BY **RANULPH FIENNES**

PAVILION

This edition published in 2010 by Pavilion Books

An imprint of Anova Books Company Ltd
10 Southcombe Street,
London, W14 0RA

First published in the United Kingdom in 2007
by Pavilion Books

Design and layout © Pavilion, 2007
Text © Kym McConnell and Dave Horsley, 2007

Commissioning Editor: Kate Oldfield
Editor: Kate Burkhalter
Designer: Austin Taylor
Jacket Design: Georgina Hewitt
Indexer: Vanessa Bird
Maps: Martin Darlison at Encompass Graphics Ltd

ISBN 9781-86205-886-6

A CIP catalogue record for this book is available from the British Library.

10 9 8 7 6 5 4 3 2 1

Reproduction by Spectrum Colour Ltd, England
Printed and bound by Toppan Leefung Printing Ltd, China

www.anovabooks.com

PAGE 1 Runners in the North Pole Marathon.

PAGES 2/3 Competitor in the world's most northerly race – the North Pole Marathon.

THIS PAGE Crossing 14km of the great salt flats in Xinjiang Province, China – the Gobi March.

PAGES 6/7 Runners spread out along Sahara desert flats – Marathon des Sables.

PAGE 8 Sir Ranulph Fiennes running strongly during the North Pole Marathon 2004.

PAGE 9 Shortly after finishing second in the North Pole Marathon.

FOR WENDY, SAMUEL AND TOBY
– **KYM**

FOR PETE
– **DAVE**

# CONTENTS

# FOREWORD

LONG DISTANCE RUNNING AND POLAR EXPLORATION are two of my passions. Both present the opportunity for challenging and enormously fulfilling experiences.

To discover a world where those passions are combined, where individuals take themselves to the extreme frontiers of the environment and their own physical capacity for endurance, is inspiring and exciting.

Many international events, organized exclusively for runners, are now being offered annually, thus providing individuals with the opportunity to explore and to challenge themselves in remote locations. Running in the Sahara, Amazon, Himalayas or the Antarctica is more accessible than ever and has never been easier to organize.

One cannot help but be impressed with ultra runners. They race continuously over periods in excess of 24, or even 48, hours. These sportspeople possess a large dose of determination and endurance.

In 2004 I was fortunate to compete in one of the races featured in this book – the North Pole Marathon. I had been at the Pole before, but this was pleasantly different in that I didn't have to haul a sled there! However, it was still a great test of fitness and stamina.

Also during our 7x7x7 Challenge (seven marathons on seven continents, in seven days) in 2003, Mike Stroud and I were pushed to our limits running in the tropical heat and humidity of Singapore.

*Extreme Running* profiles 24 of the most challenging and exciting foot races across the globe and offers readers, runners, adventurers, travellers and explorers alike, the opportunity to discover the greatest adventure running races in the world. But more than that, it empowers and inspires ordinary individuals to take on extraordinary feats and succeed.

I congratulate Kym McConnell and Dave Horsley on completing their own 7 Extreme Marathons on 7 Continents challenge and for producing this excellent reference book.

The book superbly captures the essence of running in extremes and I am sure it will inspire many others to tackle similar goals.

*Ran Fiennes*
2007.

RANULPH
**FIENNES**

# INTRODUCTION

"After gazing at the sky for some time, I came to the conclusion that such beauty had been reserved for remote and dangerous places, and that nature has good reasons for demanding special sacrifices from those who dare to contemplate it."

Richard E. Byrd, *Alone* (1938)

EXTREME RUNNING IS EMERGING AS A NEW SPORTS GENRE. The sport encompasses a class of extraordinary foot races that extend beyond the norm of running experiences. Qualifying events are of the greatest possible degree or extent or intensity: be it extreme altitude, extreme cold, extreme heat, extreme terrain, extreme remoteness and/or extreme isolation. Extreme running events may be on or off-road and of distances that vary from a single marathon to hundreds of kilometres. Events tend to require competitors to have a combination of ultra-runners' endurance, the technical skill of the adventure racer, and the innate mental and physical capacity to survive in extreme environs under exceptional conditions.

This book features 24 selected extreme running events. There are many others and with recent growth and ever-increasing publicity of extreme sports there are now races in almost every country. As our day-to-day lives become more pressured and intense, it comes as no surprise that races such as these are proliferating. According to Sir Roger Bannister:

*The more restricted our society and work becomes the more necessary it will be to find some outlet for this craving for freedom.*

People often ask what leads one to run 200 kilometres through a desert, over frozen glaciers and lakes or through remote humid tropical jungles. There are really two answers. One is the almost spiritual nature of this type of quest. Extreme running forces a separation between mind and body. The ability to reach a level of meditation that permits a runner mentally to overcome extreme environmental factors and crippling physical exertion is key. The greater and more extreme the physical challenge, then the more transcendental the experience. With this, can come a true sense of peace and escape from the everyday pressures of life.

The second answer is more base: it is the desire to succeed, to conquer, to overcome a seemingly impossible physical and mental challenge. The thrill of taking on such a mission, of believing in oneself to the necessary extent to succeed, is tantalizing. The self-confidence that many extreme runners possess is a necessary prerequisite to success. Without it, failure is almost inevitable. This is because these extremely difficult physical and psychological feats serve to highlight the frailty of the human condition. Fear of failure in itself is a difficult thing to face and to beat. Yet when self-belief is mirrored in success, the intangible rewards that result from having faced and conquered unexplored areas of physical and mental consciousness, and having probed the limits of muscular endurance, are great.

The inspiration for this book came from the authors' personal quest to complete an 'extreme footrace' on each of the seven continents. The mission was christened the '7 Continents Extreme Running Challenge'. After a careful

deliberation and selection process, a series of races was identified in order to achieve a cross-section of terrain (including snow, ice, jungle and desert), altitude (up to 5184m (17,000ft)) and climate (with temperatures ranging from -30°C to 56°C (-22°F to 133°F)). The single constant is that each and every one of these races is extreme in nature. Multiple events around the world were identified, and a large proportion of these tested, and the toughest and most unique are included herein.

The book profiles the best three or four 'extreme footraces' on each continent. The featured events are accessible and achievable, each being an organized event, which participants are able to enter relatively easily. 'Unorganized' runs, such as the Grand Canyon Traverse (US) or the Triple Peaks Challenge (UK), have been omitted. The book also contains only those events that are held on an annual basis, thus excluding ad hoc events such as the Race Across America or Trans-Europe Footrace. Standard road/track races are also excluded, including the world's longest certified race – Sri Chinmoy's 3,100 Mile Race.

The 24 races in the book can be categorized as follows:

**Ultra-marathons** Badwater Ultramarathon, Comrades Marathon, Spartathlon

**Ultra-trails** Ultra-Trail du Tour du Mont-Blanc, Kepler Challenge, Wasatch Front 100 Miler, Verdon Canyon Challenge, Le Grand Raid, Trans 333, Yukon Arctic Ultra, Te Houtaewa Challenge, Bogong to Hotham Trail Run

**Trail/Mountain Marathons** Everest Marathon, Antarctica Marathon, Inca Trail Marathon, Pikes Peak Marathon, Lake Baikal International Ice Marathon, Antarctic Ice Marathon, North Pole Marathon

**Multi-stage Footraces** Marathon des Sables, Jungle Marathon, Gobi March, Atacama Crossing, Transalpine-Run

NORTH POLE
MARATHON

ARCTIC OCEAN

YUKON ARCTIC
ULTRA

LAKE BAIKAL
INTERNATIONAL
ICE MARATHON

ULTRA-TRAIL DU TOUR
DU MONT-BLANC    TRANSALPINE-RUN

WASATCH FRONT
100 MILER    PIKES PEAK
BADWATER    MARATHON
ULTRAMARATHON

VERDON CANYON
CHALLENGE    SPARTATHLON

GOBI
MARCH

MARATHON
DES SABLES

EVEREST
MARATHON

ATLANTIC
OCEAN

TRANS
333

PACIFIC
OCEAN

PACIFIC
OCEAN

JUNGLE
MARATHON

INDIAN
OCEAN

INCA TRAIL
MARATHON

ATACAMA
CROSSING

LE GRAND
RAID DE LA
RÉUNION

BOGONG TO
HOTHAM
TRAIL RUN

TE HOUTAEWA
CHALLENGE

COMRADES
MARATHON

KEPLER
CHALLENGE

ANTARCTICA
MARATHON

ANTARCTIC ICE
MARATHON

These extreme runs include the highest, lowest, most southerly, most northerly, hottest and coldest, footraces on the planet. They take place in the most remote corners of the globe — such as the Sahara, the Himalayas, the Amazon, and both the Antarctic and Arctic Circles.

Competing in and against these conditions and environments brings individual runners closer to the land and environs than any other form of travel: that in itself brings an incredibly rich and rewarding experience. At the end of the day, these events are less about the running course and more about the very personal journey within oneself.

PAGE 10 Crossing one of the many mountain passes in the Alps — Transalpine-Run.
PAGE 11 Running amongst Fiordland peaks in the deep south of New Zealand — Kepler Challenge.
OPPOSITE Blazing a trail through the swampy Amazon rainforest — Jungle Marathon.
ABOVE *Extreme Running* profiles the best 'extreme footraces' on each continent.

## "The only true wisdom lives far from mankind, out in the great loneliness, and can be reached only through suffering."
**Igjugarjuk, Caribou Eskimo Shaman**

1

# ULTRA-TRAIL DU TOUR
## DU MONT-BLANC

**PAGES 14/15** Competitors cling to the rock face between Steeg and St Anton on the Transalpine-Run.
**THIS PAGE** Stunning views of Mont-Blanc from the Col de la Seigne (2,516m) that marks the French/Italian border.

THE ULTRA-TRAIL DU TOUR DU MONT-BLANC (UTMB) is much more than an extreme foot race. It is a unique and unrivalled traverse through the cultural and ecological diversity of the Alps, that magnificent mountain range which stretches from France in the west to Slovenia in the East.

Other extreme foot race courses also take competitors through spectacularly beautiful, yet often hostile and unpredictable, alpine terrain and conditions, including the Everest Marathon and the Kepler Challenge. But the novel and unparalleled feature of the UTMB is that terrain which should be remote and inaccessible is, in fact, right in the centre of thriving and relatively heavily populated Western Europe. Moreover, the race itself takes place in a busy month in the European summer and meanders through various tourist hotspots — in France, Italy and Switzerland.

The Alps form a daunting, but not impossible, barrier between some of the commercial centres of Europe. For hundreds of years, traders, adventurers, soldiers, pilgrims and, latterly, tourists, have crossed its various passes by foot. This pedestrain traffic has shaped these mountains and created a bespoke trail, complete with permanent aid stations, for the ideal 160+km extreme running event.

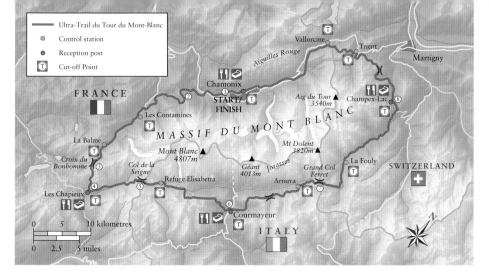

The UTMB route ventures from Chamonix valley to Courmayeur, then Val Ferret to Bovine along the French, Italian and Swiss foothills. The trail meanders through pastures and creeps up to the glistening glaciers and awesome peak views as it winds over various passes, including Col du Bonhomme, Col de la Seigne and Grand Col Ferret. Throughout this 163km odyssey, nature puts on a spectacular display.

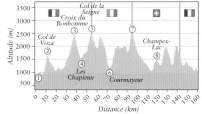

The multicultural mix of hosts honour competitors with a consistent stream of unsurpassed hospitality and support. The enthusiasm and kindness is simply unequalled. For centuries, the people who live in these mountain ranges have assisted and saved the foot soldiers who have passed by day and night. The UTMB is just another chapter in the extraordinarily accommodating lives of these people in their wonderful communities.

*'I was encouraged by the public all the way. I have never done a race with such a friendly and motivating public. It was wonderful!'*

MARCO OLMO (2006 RACE WINNER)

# 'Circumnavigating the highest and most spectacular mountain massif in Western Europe, the Tour du Mont Blanc takes walkers right to the foot of the towering rock faces and glaciers where alpinism was born.'

*Walking in the Alps*, Lonely Planet (2004)

Yet like their predecessors of a by-gone era, the competitors in the UTMB must still endure in many ways the extremeties of the alpine environment alone and largely unassisted. They must navigate the terrain, manage their own physical condition and retain the mental endurance that it takes to overcome the challenges of this extreme event.

## A European Odyssey

The UTMB is the only extreme running race in the world to take place across the territory of three different countries in a single, uninterrupted stage. It is a 163km adventure through the Pays du Mont Blanc (the country of Mont Blanc, the magnificent massif that dominates this region of Europe). It takes competitors

**BELOW** Departing from the Triangle de l'Amitié Square in the centre of Chamonix.

'HOW DID THIS BEAUTIFUL ADVENTURE BEGIN?'

It is the story of a group of friends and their shared passions: passions for their magnificent Mont Blanc country, for nature, for the people of the Region... We wanted to share a dream rather than just a sporting event and to offer others the opportunity to live a veritable human adventure full of encounters.

The Mont Blanc range's reputation as a tourist attraction requires no introduction. It stems from the varied scenery which its hills and peaks, glaciers, valleys and villages have to offer, but also from the varied peoples of the region.

Embarking on a tour of Mont Blanc is a little like embarking on a journey around the world! 3 countries are united around a mythical mountain, a hymn to the diversity of its people and its scenery. The union respects their strong human values [respect (for the environment and the people), for sharing and solidarity, knowledge of oneself....)].

Runners travel from all over the world to participate in this adventure. There are many volunteers (over 1000), who come not only to help, but also to be part of the celebration. The emotional dimension of their desire to participate (either by running or as volunteers) is a very important aspect of their involvement. It is as if each and every participant seizes an opportunity to better themselves. A large majority of the runners go beyond mere sport in their commitment, they run for a cause: they run to get over a serious illness, they run for someone close in great difficulty and for many charitable organizations. For the vast majority of people, finishing this race is like getting to the end of a quest for the holy grail.

This race is distinctive and the essential character of The North Face Ultra-Trail du Tour du Mont-Blanc undoubtedly centres on its geography (the Mont Blanc massif). But it lies yet more certainly in the race's rare emotional dimension!

**Catherine Poletti**
RACE DIRECTOR

through France, Italy and Switzerland, crossing six major mountain passes, ascending a total height of 8,900m.

The real challenge is that this epic journey must be completed in less than 46 hours. Competitors are monitored at the 10 checkpoints along the route, and if they fail to make the various stage cut-off times, they are pulled from the event. Those who remain — 40 per cent ultimately — will face the daunting prospect of running for up to 20 hours in total darkness. It is not just dark, it is coal-black and the meagre light of a single headlamp does little to illuminate the precarious way underfoot.

Pays du Mont Blanc is a marvellous place with stunning peaks, gorges, waterfalls, glaciers, lakes and nature reserves. Competitors pass them all, but under the heavy cloak of darkness may miss a few.

**ABOVE LEFT** Race registration – collecting race numbers and drop-bags.

The race follows, for the most part, the famous Tour du Mont Blanc trekking route through seven valleys in the Pays du Mont Blanc: Arve, Monjoie, des Glaciers, Veni, two Vals Ferret (one Italian, one Swiss) and Vallée du Triente. Each valley has its own special character and features. Towering above the valleys are the mighty peaks of the ranges.

*'This is "the" famous long-distance walk in the Alps, and the Tour du Mont Blanc has got it all: fine views, variety of terrain and scenery, different*

**RACE** The North Face Ultra-Trail du Tour du Mont-Blanc

**LOCATION** Mont Blanc massif (France, Italy, Switzerland)

**DISTANCE** 163km (101mile), single stage (86km) race also available)

**DATE** Late August

**TOTAL ASCENT** 8900m (29,200ft)

**TOTAL DESCENT** 8900m (29,200ft)

**KEY CHARACTERISTICS** Run around famous Tour du Mont Blanc trail in less than 46 hours, start/finish in Chamonix. Pass through France, Italy and Switzerland - crossing 6 passes over 2,000m (6,562ft) high

**RACE RECORDS** Course varies slightly each year

**FIELD (APPROX)** Limited to 2000

**CLIMATE** May be very cold during the night stages (particularly at altitude)

**FINISHERS** 40–45% of starters

**RACE DIRECTORS** Catherine & Michel Poletti

**EMAIL** info@autmb.com

**WEB** www.ultratrailmb.com

*countries, high passes, beautiful Alpine valleys…this is the yardstick by which all others are measured.'*

HILLARY SHARP, *TREKKING AND CLIMBING IN THE WESTERN ALPS*, GLOBE TROTTER ADVENTURE GUIDES (2002)

The Tour du Mont Blanc is the most popular long trek in Europe with more than 25,000 trekkers passing through each summer. The route typically takes 9-10 days and traditionally begins in Les Houches (7km on from Chamonix). The first recorded trekking group set out from Chamonix in 1767 with Horace-Bénédict De Saussure, a wealthy Swiss scientist, together with an entourage of guides, porters and mules. He described it as follows: *'the majestic glaciers, separated by great forests and crowned by granite rocks which rise to incredible heights, offer one of the most magnificent and impressive sights imaginable'.*

Central to the region and the route is, of course, the Mont Blanc massif. At 4,808m, Mont Blanc dominates the range and its summit rises at least 3,700m above the township of Chamonix, and wears the crown of Monarch of the Alps.

*'Mont Blanc is the Monarch of mountains;*
*They crowned him long ago,*
*On a throne of rocks – in a robe of clouds –*
*With a Diadem of Snow.'*

LORD BYRON, *MANFRED* (1817)

The UTMB race was probably born in 1978, when Frenchmen Christian Roussel and Jacky Duc completed a self-sufficient run around the TMB trail. They set off after work one evening, without any particular preparations, and returned after 24 hours 50 minutes. The men then looked to improve the run by utilising better logistical support. Duc withdrew and was substituted with the 28-year-old Swiss, Jacques Berlie, for the second attempt.

On that second attempt, Roussel and Berlie set out from Chamonix and 10 friends provided pre-planned food and liquid supplies and support en route. The exercise went to plan and the two men successfully completed the course in

21 hours 48 minutes. This new 'record' was to remain the benchmark until the first official UTMB in 2003.

## Getting In To Chamonix

Chamonix is an ancient and beautiful mountain town that has long been a lay-over for travellers to the region. Nowadays it is a destination in itself. It is commonly pronounced the world's greatest climbing centre and offers adventurers all manner of experiences. It is, above all else, the closest town to the base of Mont Blanc and has prospered as a result of the lure of the summit. As early as 1800, Chamonix became a tourist centre. Alpinism − the sport of mountaineering − was virtually invented there.

With an adventure pedigree like it has, Chamonix is a natural and irresistible starting point to the UTMB race. It is a bustling tourist town with plentiful resources. And it needs them, given the ever-increasing popularity of the race. Its numbers peaked at 2,500 in 2006. The race organizers are still trying to balance this extraordinary demand with the environmental impact of such a massive field. In 2007, the quota (reduced back to 2,000) was reached within 10 hours of

**BELOW** Passing Glacier de Miage near the remains of Lake Combal.

applications opening online. Heavy demand is expected to continue with competitors registering from 48 nations.

## The Four Phases of the Race

The UTMB Race course naturally splits into four sections – centred on the principal 'reception posts' at Chamonix, Les Chapieux, Cormayeur and Lake Champex. Competitors are able mentally to dissect the trail into a series of near marathon-length stages. Each has its own peculiar challenges in terms of terrain and elevation profile, but it is somehow more manageable to have a general idea of what each stage means in terms of distance.

Cormayeur and Lake Champex are the locations where runners' 'drop bags' are 'dropped' by race support crew. 'Drop bags' contain fresh clothes and food provisions packed by the competitors beforehand and can provide the necessities required to freshen up and fill up. In addition, race organizers provide hot meals and sheltered sleeping facilities if required, at these two sites.

## PHASE ONE – CHAMONIX TO LES CHAPIEUX

*The distance from Chamonix to Les Chapieux is 44km and there is an 11-hour cut-off time. The route involves crossing two significant passes: Col de Voza at 1,635m with its 650m ascent; and Croix du Bonhomme at 2,479m with its 1,270m ascent.*

The race starts at 7pm from the Triangle de l'Amitié Square in Chamonix, based at the pleasant altitude of 1,035m. Crowds of well-wishers are amassed along the streets of the town, cheering on the competitors as they set off into the fading light.

From Chamonix, it is a gentle run down the right hand side of the Arve valley floor to Les Houches (8km), passing by the Les Gaillands climbing school, which is the first in the world. The flat terrain is in stark contrast to the 650m climb from Les Houches to Col de Voza at 1,653m (13km). Competitors take refreshments after Col de Voza and then set off into the pitch dark of the night as it descends at around 9pm.

After nightfall, the trail is lit up by a snake of 2,000 headlights lining the mountain slopes. The glittering snake quickly descends into Bionnassay and then further down the Val Montjoie to Les Contamines at a height of 1,150m (25km).

**ABOVE** A runner stretching at a 'TMB' signpost.

The 25km mark is also the first of the ten 'control station' (or time checkpoints) along the course. It is still relatively early in the evening, at least for the French, and the town is alight with a street-party atmosphere in the town square. It is a warm and reinvigorating welcome for the runners coming in from the lonely night.

Before too long, competitors must set off again, leaving the street revellers behind. It is approximately a further 4km to the celebrated baroque chapel of Notre Dame de la Gorge, which is a little difficult to see in the dark. From there, it is a 300m climb up a Roman-built paved mule path aptly called the 'Roman Way'. It was built from flagstones approximately 2,000 years ago. The path leads to a hanging valley and the Balme refuge (hut) at the 33km mark for refreshments at the

**RIGHT** Medical volunteers assisting a runner at the Cormayeur reception post.

second control station. From there, it is onwards and upwards to the Col du Bonhomme, then a further climb towards the Col de la Croix du Bonhomme at 2,483m. There is a refuge on south side of the saddle at the 38km mark, before a rapid descent into the Vallee des Glaciers. The 900m drop into the valley includes several treacherous ravine crossings before reaching the safe haven of the tiny hamlet of Les Chapieux at 1,549m (44km). This is the first of the four reception posts and marks the end of phase one.

In true mountain folk style, the 'middle of the night' reception is bursting with hospitality. The La Nova refuge is a big tent with hot meals, masseuses and an opportunity to rest. It is too cold for competitors to linger for too long and besides there are still three more marathons to go.

## RACING THE CLOCK:

THERE IS ONE ASPECT of preparation for the UTMB that requires significant forethought and strategic consideration: time management.

Due to the extraordinarily strict cut-off times, enforced vigilantly at each control station (check point), finishing this race is not simply a matter of being able to cover the 163km distance. It must be done in less than 46 hours. And 55 – 60 per cent of participants fail to do so.

Of those competitors who do complete the entire loop around Mont Blanc and back to Chamonix, almost half take between 40–46 hours to do so. Therefore, the entire event is an exercise of finely tuned time management. The majority of the field is constantly focused on staying ahead of time and, as such, will vary (lengthen or shorten) anticipated rest breaks at each of the 10 cut-off checkpoints in order to keep within self-imposed time limits. This is particularly true for the principal 'reception posts' at Chapieux, Cormayeur and Lake Champex, where a planned duration for a rest break (at these locations) may vary by up to one hour depending on progress.

One quarter of the field is timed out before or at Cormayeur, and a further quarter is timed out before or at Lake Champex. Yet of the remaining competitors who continue beyond Lake Champex, more than 90 per cent will complete the circular course into Chamonix.

## PHASE TWO – LES CHAPIEUX TO CORMAYEUR

*This is a distance of 28km, with a 7-hour cut-off time. The route entails two well-spaced passes — Col de la Seigne at 2,516m and Arète du Mont-Favre at 2,435m — giving no respite from the incessant ascent and descent of the trail. At some point in the night, competitors leave France and enter Italy.*

It is 4.5km from Les Chapieux to La Ville des Glacier (1,779m). En route there are three or four farms, which competitors hear and smell rather than see. From the farm it is a short distance to Refuge des Mottets. It is then a 4km, steep and arduous ascent to Col de la Seigne (2,516m) at the 54km mark. The climb starts with a dozen big hairpin turns in the trail and ends on the col that marks the Italian border. The col provides one of the best views of Mont Blanc along the UTMB. Unfortunately, for most of the competitors it is not yet sunrise, so the view is somewhat limited.

It can be freezing cold at the Col de la Siegne and competitors are keen rapidly to drop down into the upper reaches of Val Veni, to Refuge Elizabetta, perched high at 2,200m. The hut marks the 58km mark and the fourth control station. From there, it is a gentle descent on a wide 4WD track to the remains of Lake Combal, which is flanked by the Miage Glacier moraine. Then it is a 450m climb up to Montfavre ridge at 2,435m altitude (62.8km). From the ridge, the route descends down to Col Checrouit and the Maison Vieille refuge at 1,953 metres (67km).

The twisting path from the Maison Vieille takes competitors down a steep ski slope into Courmayeur, where the second reception post is based at the local Dolonne Sports Centre and a much more sensible altitude of 1,190m. The second reception post marks 72km and is the psychological half-way point in the race. It is a delightful town, Italy's answer to Chamonix. It is smaller, but warmer. The two villages are no longer separated by 72 kilometres of mountain trail. Since the mid-1960s, residents have been connected by the 16km Mont Blanc tunnel. Courmayeur is known for its mineral springs and is an ideal location for the reception post's offering of shelter, hot food, medical support and mattresses. Competitors are also reunited with their first 'drop bags' and can partake in any treats that they packed before setting off the night before.

**BELOW** Crossing over the Mont-Favre ridge (2,435m).

## PHASE THREE – CORMAYEUR TO CHAMPEX-LAC

*The third phase is the longest of the race at 45km, with a seemingly generous 14-hour cut-off time. The elite runners finish this stage in well under 7 hours. Although there is just one pass in the third phase, there are two notable climbs – the steep 800m ascent out of Cormayuer and the 670m climb up the Grand Col Ferrat at 2,537m, which marks the highest point on the course.*

Runners leave Cormayer with a steep climb up Mont de la Saxe to Bertone hut at 1,989m (77km). Above the refuge is a long grassy ridge and excellent running (all in daylight) for the next 11km. This point is famed for being the best viewpoint for south side of Mont Blanc massif, including the Grandes Jorasses and other nearby peaks across Val Ferrat. After some excellent running, the trail eventually descends to Refuge Bonatti (2,020m, 84km), named after celebrated Italian mountaineer Walter Bonatti. After the hut is a drop through rare, lush vegetation to the bed of Val Ferrat at Arnuva (1,769m, 89km) and the fifth control station.

From the control station, competitors head up to Refuge Elena at the head of valley. Above Elena is the Grand Col Ferret at 2,537m (93km) and the Italian/Swiss border. To the left is Mont Dolent (the 'triple frontier'), which dominates the horizon and is symbolic of this tri-cultural event. The descent to the idyllic Swiss Val Ferrat, marking the eastern extent of Mont Blanc range, is through beautiful pasture land. The route then stays low with less grandiose views but gentler terrain to the pretty mountain town of La Fouly (1,593m, 102km) and the sixth control station. Competitors are encouraged to savour the local fare and, in particular, the Swiss cheese raclette.

**BELOW TOP** Competitors taking refreshments at the Col de Voza as night falls.
**BOTTOM** The middle of the night inside Les Chapieux refuge tent (after 44km).

From La Fouly is another 500m drop to the northern end of valley, where the trail then ascends 500m through peaceful forest to emerge at the lakeside resort of Champex (1,466m, 117km) and the third reception post. The reception post is situated inside an old World War II artillery fort, which is somehow fitting for the battered foot soldiers arriving at its doors. Here awaits the second 'drop bag' and its welcome and much anticipated contents. This is the place to get some rest, assuming that there is time, and the underground 'bunkers' can provide a surprisingly welcome retreat.

## PHASE FOUR – CHAMPEX-LAC TO CHAMONIX

*The last leg is the final 41km from Champex-Lac back to Chamonix with a cut-off time of 13 hours. Two final passes await near Bovine (1,987m) and Les Tseppes (1,932m), the steepest climb on the course and where competitors return to France.*

The fourth phase route is a delightful variety of woodland and alpine pasture. The day offers up magnificent views over the Rhône valley and Lake Geneva (but only in the daylight). The exhausting ascent up to the Portalo collar at 2,040m is rewarded with the spectacular views down the Vallee du Trient and a rapid descent to Trient (1,279m, 132km) and the seventh control station.

From Trient awaits one of the steepest slopes on the course. It is a 700m ascent over the course of 3km to the picturesque Tseppes chalet at 1,932m. The chalet is directly opposite the magnificent Trient Glacier. From there, it is a further 150m climb to the pass and then another quick drop down to the Catogne pastures. The descent continues to the chair lift station at Les Esserts (1,640m, 140km). Finally, competitors are back on French soil.

The road then leads 1.5km down into Vallorcine (1,260m, 142km) and the ninth control station. From there, it is a gentle climb up the old coach paths to Col des Montets, which brings competitors parallel to the L'Arve valley road. The course crosses the main road at the town of Argentière (1,260m, 149km) before starting the final 10km 'sprint', including one final 110m climb before the descent into Chamonix.

**ABOVE** Bravissimo! Chamonix finish line – every runner has his or her own unique race story.

## An Emotional End:

Like with so many extreme running races, completing the UTMB is an emotional experience. The final 500m leading into Chamonix are alive with the resounding cheers of admiration and applause from the waiting crowd and the enthusiastic and ever-supportive cries of bravissimo!

> 'The night was very testing. At Les Chapieux, I wanted to retire. My legs were giving way, and my mind too. It was my friends who encouraged me. The magnificent scenery, the surrounding mountains and the solitude of my running pushed me on. I was finally OK!'
> CHRISTOPHE JAQUEROD (2005 RACE WINNER)

# VERDON CANYON
# **CHALLENGE**

THE VERDON GORGE is 20km long and more than 300m deep. Sheer limestone
cliffs rise from the river bed in the canyon floor, making this an awesome and
intimidating setting. The Verdon Canyon Challenge 'Ultrail' takes runners on a
100km journey up, down and across this incredible rift that has been carved out of
the plain by the Verdon River. The gradient changes are severe, the temperatures
are oppressive and the 30 hour cut-off time is testing, making this a race that will
challenge even the hardiest mountain man or woman.

The race is based from the village of Aiguines (837m), set above Lake Sainte-
Croix. This small holiday village boasts quaint narrow lanes and a gentle street café
culture. Outside the village, the gorge dominates the entire landscape and the race.
Its sides are steep and the trails down it are narrow. The roads on either side cling
perilously close to the edge, contouring high above the meandering river below.

# 'The Verdon is certainly one of the most spectacular places in France.'

**Dominic Chauvelier (four time French national marathon champion)**

## KEY DATA

**RACE** Verdon Canyon Challenge 'Ultrail'
**LOCATION** Gorges du Verdon (Aiguines, France)
**DISTANCE** 100km (62 miles), single stage
**DATE** June
**TOTAL ASCENT** 6,030m (19,780ft)
**TOTAL DESCENT** 6,030m (19,780ft)
**KEY CHARACTERISTICS** Steep, rocky, narrow trails in Europe's largest canyon – the Verdon Gorge.
**RACE RECORDS** Male 8:39, Female 12:02 (70km course)
**FIELD (APPROX)** 40
**CLIMATE** Day: 38°C (100°F); Night: 10°C (50°F)
**FINISHERS** 85–90% of starters
**RACE DIRECTOR** Jean Giacosa
**EMAIL** contact@aeria.fr
**WEB** www.aeria.fr

The footpaths zigzag down into the gorge, making it difficult to assess the distance covered. It seems to take forever to arrive at the bottom, and the climb out the other side is foreboding.

Race participants face multiple treacherous sections on this challenging route, including the gnarly Sentier de l'Imbut (meaning 'Funnel Path'). The trail shrinks away to rock ledges, requiring competitors to scramble, protected only by steel cable handholds. From the Funnel Path, the route heads directly up to a long trail of steeply carved steps, barely 30cm wide, to the cliff top.

The steepest in a series of steep descents in this race is a 350m vertical drop from the popular lookout at La Maline chalet, down to the Estellie footbridge. Down here, the heat is trapped, and the atmosphere is stifling. Despite the presence of the turquoise coloured river, dehydration is a serious issue; aid stations are relatively scarce and set far apart in the race. A second, equally energy-sapping section, is the ascent up to the high point at Le Grand Margès (1,577m), which is challenging in the extreme.

The Verdon Canyon Challenge 'Ultrail' is a young race but built on the foundation of the original three-day event that has been running for over 14 years. The new 100km single stage race option is set to become one of the top ultra-trail elite races in Europe. Race Director, Jean Giacosa, neatly sums up the essence of this small but special event: '*A great race is not judged by the number of participants but by its organisation and its aura.*'

# TRANSALPINE-**RUN**

THE TRANSALPINE-RUN involves a mind-boggling cumulative ascent of almost 14,000m, rendering it one of the most vertically challenged races on the long distance running event calendar. This extraordinary feat is performed amid the spectacular backdrop of alpine scenery located in temperate and accessible Europe.

The Transalpine-Run is a multi-stage foot race. Unlike many other extreme running events, competitors are not required to be self-sufficient or to provide their own support crews. Support is provided along the course and race accommodations are extremely comfortable. That said, the race is still one of the most arduous, and in places remote, events in the world. Stages of extreme isolation mean that for safety reasons runners are required to compete in teams of two and are required to carry mandatory safety gear.

**ABOVE** Participants must compete in teams of two, running together throughout the race.

Competitors are not, however, required to carry all of their equipment and supplies for the entire multi-day event. And, as they are unencumbered by heavy packs, competitors are able to cover the 30–40km stages relatively quickly, despite the never ending ascents and descents. The longest stage (over 32km) has a cut-off time of just six-and-a-half hours, which most competitors achieve comfortably.

There are eight stages in total. At the end of each stage, teams are either billeted by local townspeople, sleep communally on the local sports hall floor, or check into local hotels. Outside the comfortable overnight stops, there are checkpoints every seven to 10km along the course. The daily routine for the eight-day event begins with breakfast and a comprehensive briefing to discuss the route for the next stage. Inevitably, the route will involve some climbing. Just one stage involves nothing but climbing: stage six is a 930m hill climb out of Scuol (Switzerland) to the top of the local cable car.

The trail can be treacherous and there is serious risk of injury. Most competitors carry trekking poles to help to steady their balance on the more difficult sections. The terrain varies from wide farm roads to narrow, rocky mountain passes and the typical challenges of alpine terrain and rocky trails.

## KEY DATA

**RACE** Transalpine-Run
**LOCATION** German, Austrian, Swiss & Italian Alps
**DISTANCE** 230km (142 miles), 8 stages.
**DATE** September
**TOTAL ASCENT** 14,000m (45,930ft)
**TOTAL DESCENT** 13,300m (43,630ft)
**KEY CHARACTERISTICS** Alpine foot race, across four countries, for teams of 2 over mountain tracks and country roads
**RACE RECORDS** Male 25:35, Female 34:33, Mixed 31:46
**FIELD (APPROX)** Limited to 300 teams
**CLIMATE** Day: 30°C (86°F); Night: 0°C (32°F)
**FINISHERS** 80–85% of starting teams
**RACE DIRECTOR** Uta Albrecht
**EMAIL** info@planb-event.com
**WEB** www.transalpine-run.com

# 'Some men storm imaginary Alps all their lives, and die in the foothills cursing difficulties which do not exist.'

**Edward W. Hore**

Throughout the event, local communities come out in support of the participants. In the various small mountain towns en route, the oompah bands play inspiring mountain music. There is a distinct, carnival-like atmosphere throughout the race, which is in force at the finishing line of each stage. A large support entourage travels from town to town to ensure that the runners receive the support and encouragement that they need and deserve.

Overall, the Transalpine-Run is a truly epic adventure. The reward is in the stunningly beautiful vistas that surround the course and the very special community spirit that develops amongst its participants.

**BELOW** Approaching the top of the Val d'Uina canyon, the border between Switzerland and Italy.

# SPARTATHLON

SPARTATHLON IS ONE of the most significant ultra-distance foot races in the world due to its extraordinary provenance and history. The event begins at the ancient Acropolis in Greece and retraces the route that historians believe the Greek messenger of legend, Pheidippides (or Philippides), took in 490BC to deliver Athen's request for reinforcements to resist the Persian invaders. In an effort to be faithful to the original, ancient feat of Pheidippides, race organizers commence the event at the same time of day that he was believed to have left Athens, at 7am. The course cut-off time is an extremely tough 36 hours.

Despite the modernization of the Greek road system, which has introduced significant stretches of smooth tarmac, the course remains challenging and the time limits are demanding. Some 250 competitors set out each year to emulate Pheidippides' achievement, but fewer than a third make it to the finish, despite the daunting pre-qualification standards applied to all applicants.

Competitors must have completed a 100km race in less than 10 hours 30 minutes, or a 200km race. It is a measure of the difficulty of the race that so many well-qualified participants fail to make Sparta within the cut off time. Pheidippides clearly set a blistering pace (without the advantage of carbo-loading, isotonic drinks or energy bars), but then his nation's survival depended upon his speed and success.

The pioneer for the modern Spartathlon race was John Foden, a British RAF Wing Commander. Foden extensively researched the route taken by Pheidippides. He and four other RAF runners completed a similar course in 1982, to prove it could be done in under 36 hours. Foden subsequently organized the first official Spartathlon race in 1983.

OPPOSITE A lone runner passes by the ancient Temple of Apollo near Corinth.

## KEY DATA

RACE  Spartathlon
LOCATION  Athens–Sparta (Peloponnese, Greece)
DISTANCE  245.3km (152 miles), single stage
DATE  September
TOTAL ASCENT  1,500m (4,920ft)
TOTAL DESCENT  1,500m (4,920ft)
KEY CHARACTERISTICS  The original ultramarathon from Athens to Sparta
RACE RECORDS  Male 20:25, Female 28:10
FIELD (APPROX)  300
CLIMATE  25–30°C (77–86°F), high probability of rain
FINISHERS  30–35% of starters
RACE DIRECTOR  Panagiotis Tsiakiris
EMAIL  spartathlon@freemail.gr
WEB  www.spartathlon.gr

'Philippides…after being sent by the generals…reached Sparta on the second day out from Athens.'

**Herodotus (recounted in *The Histories*, circa 449BC)**

From the magnificent Acropolis of ancient Athens, the police escort competitors through the streets of Athens towards the sea. The route undulates along the coastal road to the spectacular Corinth Canal (after 78.5km). It passes high over the water, and turns inland towards Corinth and less populated olive groves and farmland. At the ancient Temple of Apollo, competitors head into the hills and the citrus orchards. By the half-way mark, almost 100 runners fall by the wayside.

The survivors continue to the village of Lyrika, then into the remote countryside. Rough trails lead to a steep ascent of some 960m up to the Sangas Pass at 1,110m on Mount Parthenio. The path was designed for mountain goats, not fatigued runners, and can be dangerous. Typically, competitors reach the steep climb around midnight. The trail is marked out only by battery-driven lights. The race founder, John Fodden, did not have the same luxury: *'When we reached the pass we had to individually find our way over it without any aids except the moonlight shining on stones polished by shepherd's boots over the centuries.'*

The decent from the pass is equally challenging, and competitors must pick up the pace on the relative flat run into Netsani, in order to reach checkpoint 52 before the cut-off time.

The flat plains of Triplois follow but *'although only 50km from Sparta it is still a heartbreaking slog, often in the unrelenting heat of the new day.'* Then there is a

## GREEK LEGENDS: FROM PHEIDIPPIDES TO KOUROS

PHEIDIPPIDES' 245KM RUN from Athens to Sparta in less than two days was an incredible achievement given he was probably wearing nothing more than sandals. Sadly, the sought-after battle reinforcements were not forthcoming and he was sent back to Athens again – thus completing the first Athens–Sparta–Athens ultra-marathon.

The first official Spartathlon race, involving 45 competitors from 11 countries, was comfortably won by an unknown local called Yiannis Kouros. Kouros retained his title in 1984. His incredible finishing time of 20 hours 25 minutes remains the benchmark today. Kouros cemented his place as the greatest ever modern day ultra-runner in 1997, by setting a 24-hour track record of 305.5km (188 miles). At the time, Kourus stated: *'I will run no more 24-hour races. This record will stand for centuries'.*

In 2005, Kourus set out to repeat Pheidippides' original feat, leaving Athens 13 hours before the official Spartathlon start. He completed the second ever recorded Athens–Sparta–Athens run in a remarkable 53 hours and 43 minutes.

final drawn-out ascent after Tegea, where the road climbs steadily 975m over 22km. Although there are still 10km remaining, Sparta comes into view at the top. At the edge of the town, local schoolchildren meet the fatigued competitors and guide them to the centre of town and the feet of King Leonidas' Statue. Pheidippides brought his message of battle to Leonidas. Spartathlon competitors celebrate their arrival at the feet of the King by kissing them to celebrate their success. In true Olympian style, they are rewarded with olive wreaths and waters from the Evrotas River.

For many years, historians believed that Pheidippides' feat was one of myth, exaggerated over the eons of time and the numerous retelling of the story. Spartathlon has proven that the distance can be covered in 36 hours. That said, in the 24-year history of the event, less than 500 runners have done so. There is no doubt that Pheidippides would have held his own in today's modern, competitive world of ultra running. The fact that his record stood for over 2,500 years is testament to the athleticism of the ancient Olympians.

**BELOW** Runners kiss the feet of the King Leonidas' statue in Sparta to celebrate finishing the 246km journey, as Philippides did when delivering his ancient message from Athens.

# MARATHON
## DES SABLES

THE MARATHON DES SABLES (MDS), is the original and classic multi-stage foot race. It is a 'must do' event in the ultra-running event calendar.

The race is a 240km epic journey by foot through the Saharan desert. The actual course changes each year, like the shifting sands it charts. The sand is the omnipresent challenge that both defines and epitomizes this event. It is laid out like a burning sea of infinity and its particles contribute an invasive and uncomfortably abrasive element to the overall experience. So much so that, throughout the event's 20-year history, participants have developed all manner of techniques in an attempt to keep the sands at bay, or at least out of their shoes and clothes – but to no avail.

The idea for the race was conceived by Patrick Bauer in 1986. It has evolved from an elite race, attracting a small and exclusive field, to its current form, incorporating more than 700 international competitors. Now entering its 22nd year, MDS is a well-established and impressively organized event. This is precisely the impression the race director wishes to cultivate, asserting the race motto:

*'adventure without misadventure.'*

But the 'toughest foot race on earth' is by no means an easy feat.

The combination of searing heat, rationed water supplies and self-sufficiency, and the ubiquitous sand, makes this an extraordinarily difficult contest. In many ways, it is an adventure reminiscent of a by-gone era. Competitors with the latest hi-tech, lightweight gear have little, if any, advantage over those with traditional canvas sacks and plastic flip-flops. The desert environ is a great leveller, where the fittest and strongest – both physically and mentally – will prevail. This is enduringly captured in the race logo that features Patrick Graig, a competitor in the third MDS, with his face covered by a traditional Berber scarf, which is still the most favoured and successful method of protecting the face from the conditions.

Morocco is a country that conjures up images diverging from the nostalgic romance of Casablanca, to the bustling, laid back souks of Marrakech to the business-like town of Tangiers. Situated on the Mediterranean and Atlantic, the coastal areas enjoy a classic Mediterranean climate that allows agriculture to prosper. Inland, it is a quite different story, where the starkness of the northern Sahara is revealed.

Its gateway, for the purposes of the MDS, is the ancient garrison town of Ouarzazate. Ouarzazate is situated on the north western edge of the Sahara. The original MDS competitors endured a long bus ride to Ouarzazate over the Atlas Mountains. Now, most participants arrive by air. Ouarzazate is a thriving town that

# 'It's not the goal, but the way there that matters, and the harder the way, the more worthwhile the journey.'
**Wilfred Thesiger, *Arabian Sands* (1959)**

ONE MORNING IN DECEMBER 1984 an idea suddenly dawned on me following a discussion with two friends: to channel all of our energy towards the same aim, crossing the Sahara on foot.

I lived through an experience that I would like everybody to share. I know what I had to go through, what I lacked, what worked and what didn't and I wanted others to experience it.

The 'Marathon Des Sables' caters for many tastes: those seeking a sporting exploit, an act of personal daring or a desire to use the extreme and its attendant disorientation to get rid of the accumulated dross of one's everyday existence.

I have always wanted my event to enable competitors to discover little-known regions of Morocco as well as helping several other parts of the country to attract a limited form of tourism.

The desert is where the craziest, wildest and most beautiful dreams blend.

**Patrick Bauer**
RACE DIRECTOR

[1]All extracts taken from *Marathon Des Sables*, Patrick Bauer et al (Editions SPE, 2000)

**ABOVE** The Ahansal brothers lead the way, encouraged by some Touareg riders.

**OPPOSITE** Cautious first steps as fully laden participants contemplate the days ahead.

makes its living off tourism and the film industry. As a consequence, it boasts a number of luxury hotels and charming cafes. Amidst its relative luxury, competitors enjoy the delicious local cuisine and culture prior to the race. What they may not yet realize is that this little town will seem a true oasis when it is re-entered at the end of the 240km epic MDS. But for the next seven days, Ouarzazate will be no more than a distant mirage-like memory, as MDS participants turn to face the full force of the Sahara Desert.

## First Sandy Saharan Steps

The day before the race, competitors board buses in Ouarzazate and are driven from there to the end of the road — literally. The tarmac gives way to sand and army vehicles replace the buses. These vehicles were not designed for comfort and there is standing room only for the short ride that plunges participants deep into the interior of the Sahara. The only way out is by foot, across a 240km barrier of sand plains and dunes.

The army vehicles drop competitors at the first campsite, known in race parlance as 'the bivouac'. The bivouac is comprised of two separate elements. There are the well-constructed, modern tents that have electricity and shower facilities. These are for the race organizers and support crews. Once the race has begun, competitors are forbidden to enter the support area. Then there are the black, Berber-style nomad tents made of a single blanket stretched over a couple of wooden poles, without electricity and ablutions to be performed in the wide, open desert. These makeshift tents each provide a home to nine competitors. They are not vast and so, when one occupant rolls over in the night, all occupants roll over. It makes sleep a challenge.

Despite the austere conditions, competitors do come to see the bivouac as a place of sanctuary. All fundamental needs are catered for within its boundaries — albeit only because they have been carried there on the competitor's own back. There is shelter and food and, most crucially, water (rationed, of course). And there are the MASH-like facilities of 'Doctrotter' to mend (or, at least, patch) the wounds inflicted by the day's ordeal.

Overall, competitors' tents are mostly amiable places and many sport the flag of the occupants' nation or banners exhibiting the resident team names. There is a sense of an international village atmosphere, which is actively encouraged by the race organizers.

## The Race

Although the course varies year by year, the general race format remains consistent. First, runners participate in a relatively short 20km acclimatization stage. That is followed by two longer stages, each around 35km. One of those 35km stages will be dominated by dunes. The fourth stage is the longest, at around 80km. Then, for all but the slowest finishers of the 80km leg, there is some respite before the penultimate stage, which is the classic marathon distance of 42km. The final day is approximately a half marathon (13km) in distance.

**KEY DATA**

**RACE** Marathon Des Sables

**LOCATION** Sahara Desert, East Morocco

**DISTANCE** 220–240km (135–150 miles), 6 stages

**DATE** March/April

**TOTAL ASCENT** Course varies each year

**TOTAL DESCENT** Course varies each year

**KEY CHARACTERISTICS** Multi-day, self-sufficiency race through open desert on sandy trails, dried lakebeds and stony tracks; all within the Sahara Desert

**RACE RECORDS** Course varies each year

**FIELD (APPROX)** 700

**CLIMATE** Day: Up to 50°C (122°F), dry; Night: Down to 5°C (41°F)

**FINISHERS** 90–95% of starters

**RACE DIRECTOR** Patrick Bauer

**EMAIL** aoi@darbaroud.com

**WEB** www.darbaroud.com

During the race, each day begins with a natural wake-up call, which is closely followed by the support staffs' unceremonious dismantling of the tents. The first water ration of the day, 1.5 litres, is used to refill water bottles, rehydrate breakfast food and complete the necessary ablutions. This is followed by a collective briefing from the race organizer at the day's start line, immediately prior to take-off.

Along the route, competitors pass through numerous checkpoints. Medical staff monitor health and issue the permitted quantities of water. With only 9 litres allocated per day for drinking, re-hydrating food and washing, every drop must be made to count.

Water management is a vital element of the MDS. In order successfully to complete the race, competitors must allocate and preserve supplies with extreme skill and care. Competitors need to consume water at a steady rate in order to regulate the body's core temperature during extreme exertion in this amazingly hot environment. If a competitor were to run out of water before reaching the next checkzsing the runner in terms of additional weight or load. Excess empty drink bottles (and even bottle caps) are all inscribed with competitor names, to deter competitors from discarding them on the course. Heavy time penalties are enforced against anyone who does lose or drop a bottle.

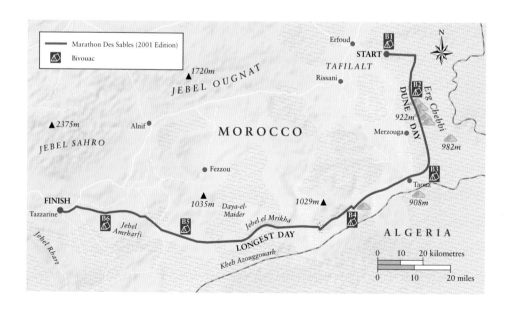

## SURVIVING STAGE ONE

The first stage of the race is deliberately short, at 20km, in order to give competitors an opportunity to acclimatize to the desert while they still have their full strength and are well hydrated. In addition, the stage permits the entire field (even the latecomers) to complete the first day in good time to reach the bivouac to wash, cook, treat injuries and prepare the following day's kit before the cold and black desert night descends.

Hygiene is critical, but the need to wash must be balanced carefully with the need to drink and eat. Many competitors deal with this dilemma by carrying antiseptic wipes but, even then, the scope for washing is limited.

Bearing in mind that this is a self-sufficient race, competitors also need to be able to heat water to re-hydrate food. To consume only cold food and drink in the evening is simply not an option, given the drastic drop in temperature in the desert at night. Therefore, most competitors carry a camp stove of some description, although the elite of the field do not. Instead, they scavenge for wood to build fires at the end of each day.

**TOP** Each runner is assigned, along with eight others, to traditional Berber-style tents for the duration of the race.

**BOTTOM** Typical kit carried by every runner, with a total weight of approximately 8-12kgs.

An aerial shot of the bivouac shows competitors in the black traditional tents with race management nearby. In the morning, runners will race through about 35km of never-ending 'dunes'.

Another tactic employed by the elite (or just savvy) members of the field is to work together in the evening preparation regime. Although each competitor must carry all of his or her own equipment, groups are allowed to work in teams within the bivouac to cook or collect water supplies. By the end of a day's running in the desert, people tend to take all the help they can get.

## DEFEATING THE DUNES

The combined effect of the difficult terrain, the searing heat and the relentless sand quickly starts to wear down competitors. The first, relatively short, day has a disproportionately wasting effect, to the alarm of first-time competitors. The knowledge that 'Dune Day' lies ahead is daunting.

The dunes rise some 1,000m from the desert floor. They form a spectacular and intimidating backdrop to the bivouac at the end of the first or second day, taunting competitors as they try to rest and unwind on the eve of 'Dune Day'.

'Dune Day' is the first real test of the competitors' strategy and equipment. The dunes themselves consist of extremely soft sand, overlaid with a relatively thin, brittle crust. Light-footed competitors are able to run along on the crust surface, especially in the lead pack. Those following — and in reality most other competitors (who are, after all, weighed down by 10kg backpacks) — crash through the crust and sink, helplessly, into the dry quicksand-like dunes. For the bulk of the competitors in the middle of the pack, the sand is churned and unstable.

The course itself meanders through the dunes for the entire day and some of the peaks are extremely high. Competitors expend valuable time and energy wading through the hostile terrain. Feet tend to sink to ankle-depth at every step. The unnatural sideways weight load on feet and joints, caused by the effort to remain upright whilst moving in a generally forward direction, is crippling. Running (or even walking) on this terrain is downright difficult. Estimates vary, but the additional

effort required to run on sand of this magnitude is approximately 30–40 per cent. Naturally, as sand rides up to mid-calf height, it is essential to have a gaiter of some description.

'Dune Day' is long and exhausting. Competitors must call upon additional reserves to conquer the steep climbs and overcome the wearing and continu-ous battle with the sand and heat. In these conditions, it is ever more impor-tant to manage water rations with great care. The consequences of running out are intensified by the conditions. The dunes are notoriously inaccessible. The innermost checkpoint support crew enter by helicopter. Therefore, evacua-tion is difficult and support through the dunes is virtually non-existent.

The only option, therefore, is for competitors to continue to rise and fall over the crests of the dunes, under the watchful eye of the beating sun. There is some comfort in the occasional glimpse from the top of the long, snaking line of runners, which meanders forward as far as the eye can see. But that is not enough to prevent exhausted and dehydrated competitors from conjuring up the mirage of the bivouac many hours before it actually comes into sight. The bivouac is worth the effort, as it is the place where competitors gratefully receive the last 4.5 litre water allocation for the day.

RIGHT 'Dune Day' – a 'crux' run stage in the MDS when competitors must negotiaite some of the highest sand dunes in the world.

## THE LONGEST DAY

If 'Dune Day' were designed to push competitors to the absolute physical and mental limit, then the 80km fourth stage of the event is almost criminal in intent. It comes hard on the (blistered) heels of 'Dune Day'. Whereas the dunes pose a seemingly insurmountable physical challenge, the psychological effect of the infamous 'Longest Day' is legendary. The distance of this fourth race stage is more

than twice the distance of any other single preceding day. For almost the entire field, it will require an element of running through the desert in the night. The sheer distance involved presents the greatest strategic challenge of the race in terms of water, food and time management.

The top 50 male and five female competitors commence the 'Longest Day' two to three hours behind the main pack. The sight of the elite packgalloping past in the searing heat with apparent ease is, perhaps surprisingly, utterly inspiring. Despite starting two to three hours behind the pack, those competitors will complete the 80km stage before sunset. The rest of the field must put this thought out of mind as the bulk of competitors prepare to spend at least part of the night out in the desert.

It is both comforting and disconcerting that one aspect of the mandatory competitor kit in the MDS is a flare. Each runner is issued with a heavy, bulky, marine-type flare, which causes almost unanimous protest at allocation. But in the deepest heart of the desert, competitors who need to use the flare are eternally grateful for its size and range. These cumbersome accessories could prove to be the difference between life and death. Disconcertingly, flares are released on a relatively common basis during the event and at least once a day. It is extraordinarily unnerving to witness the orange tongue of the flare snaking up into the sky, especially during the depths of the night on the 'Longest Day'.

At all stages in the race, support is only a flare away and will soon arrive in the form of a vehicle, if close to a checkpoint, or helicopter if necessary. The helicopters are manned by medics and are backed up by a fixed-wing aircraft, making it possible rapidly to medivac a casualty to almost anywhere in the world for treatment. There is risk, but it is a risk that is well-managed.

For those competitors who hold onto their flares, the most important decision is when to stop to rest and for how long. Temporary bivouacs are provided at the later checkpoints during the 'Longest Day' stage, but the checkpoints are busy and bustling place: not at all conducive to a short, reviving nap. It is probably more restful to sleep under the stars at the side of the trail, which can be done at any stage. But sleeping on the trail introduces even more food and water management issues and, consequently, is not an ideal solution either.

At the end of the day, and this really is the end of the day, it is just a case of getting through this stage by doing whatever it takes. If that means lying down at the side of the trail in the middle of the desert, then that is what will happen. At this stage, all focus and energy is on getting to the end of the 'Longest Day'.

## BIVOUAC BREAK AND BLISTERS

The day after the 'Longest Day' is a rest day. At least, it is a rest day for those who did not sleep out on the trail overnight and thus complete Stage 4 into the next day. The rest day provides an opportunity for reflection and contemplation – about what has transpired and what still lies ahead.

The race is by no means over. By this stage, the past few days have inevitably started to take their toll. Therefore, competitors must use the rest day to try to repair some of the damage that has been inflicted on the feet, and to rest and refuel as much as practicable.

Much needed medical assistance is provided by Doctrotter, the medical consulting group that first joined MDS in 1995. Over the years, Doctrotter's medics have developed a unique set of techniques for treating blisters in sandy conditions. What they have not devised is a method of preventing blisters altogether.

Long-distance runners do, of course, have a multitude of theories – developed over time and through experience – as to how to manage and prevent blisters. But the MDS is no ordinary long-distance run. The sustained nature of the race, combined with the heat, unusual terrain and sand, culminate to create an ideal environment for blister growth inside competitors' running shoes. The best that most competitors can do is to simply to develop a strategy for coping with their

**BELOW** Sand storms can occur at any time, making it virtually impossible to run or navigate (and difficult to keep the tent erect).

blisters, with a bit of help from Doctrotter. Doctrotter's 2005 press release stated that, in that year, *'Doctrotter treated 3,146 cases – 2,567 of which were for foot problems; used 5 kilometres of elastoplast and 125 litres of disinfectant; handed out 5,300 painkillers and 1,700 anti-inflammatories.'* Luckily for Doctrotter, whilst blisters are bothersome and, on occasion, extraordinarily painful, they are rarely life-threatening.

## MARATHON DAY

The day for rest and recuperation is agonizingly brief and, before long, competitors are limping to the start line for yet another marathon in the sand. To ultra-distance runners, a marathon is not an extraordinary event. It is almost akin to a training run. But after five gruelling days of racing in the desert, even the elite of the field are unlikely to achieve a personal best.

The end is so close (distance being entirely relative in these types of events) that few competitors withdraw after the 'Longest Day'; even fewer drop out on the final day. The final night in the bivouac brings an atmosphere of cautious, and weary, optimism. The feet, the body and the soul need to hold together for only one more day and one more half marathon.

## THE FINAL PUSH

The last stage is notionally designed to be a half marathon but, in reality, no one cares about the distance, including the race organizers. Despite the field having put behind it more than 200km of punishing effort, the pace on the final day is fast. From somewhere, deep, deep down, that last piece of energy and drive carries competitors to the final finish line.

This finish line marks the end of the run, but also the end of dehydrated food, isotonic drinks and sleeping rough. It also represents the now even more luxurious offerings of Ouarzazate. This town, that was surprisingly comfortable in the days leading up to the race, becomes a true heaven on earth at the end. The race organizer gallantly meets every finisher at the finish line and presents the finishing

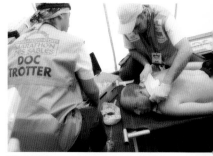

**TOP** Doctrotter medical personnel attend to needy competitors each evening – this runner has severe abrasions caused by his backpack.

**BOTTOM** The uneven terrain, heat, moisture (sweat) and sand lead to blisters and many other foot problems.

'The experience and the availability of the medical teams is essential in this domain: the classic blister can become crippling.'
**Extract from Doctrotter website.**

**ABOVE** The occasional oasis provides a welcome respite.

medals. A queue can form at peak finishing times, but this is part of the race tradition and finishers are happy to wait.

Once the MDS is finished, that flood of emotions — fears and doubts, exhilaration and amazement — is suddenly released. The adrenaline that fuelled the final miles, or in some cases the final days, seeps away, leaving raw and base exhaustion that can quickly overtake the elation that accompanies completion Competitors' thoughts rapidly turn to the most important strategic decision of the stage: how to find the bus to Ouarzazate.

## Adventure Without Misadventure

The MDS has grown from a concept that involved 23 runners taking part in the adventure of a lifetime. The event has now evolved into a sophisticated and

**LEFT** Resting at the end of the race.

**BELOW** Race Director Patrick Bauer greets every single runner as he or she crosses the finishing line.

highly organized large-scale event, but the spirit of adventure has not been lost.

Despite the extraordinarily hostile environment, and the apparent multitude of opportunities for people to get lost and things to go wrong, misadventure is simply not a feature of the MDS. Safety is paramount. Yet minimizing the risk has done nothing to detract from the enormity of the challenge. Equally, it provides no substitute for the need for any competitor to possess unsurpassed physical and mental fortitude in order to complete the event.

The satisfaction of conquering this race and this desert lasts a lifetime – long after the final blister has faded into distant memory.

## RACE HISTORY

**1984** Patrick Bauer walks 350km across the Sahara desert between Tamanrasset and In Guezam. He takes 12 days carrying a 40kg pack and has one support vehicle
**1986** 23 competitors take part in the first Marathon Des Sables between Zagora and Mhamid
**1989** A competitor (Jean-Luc Provence) collapses and subsequently dies of a heart attack
**1990** 191 competitors take part in the 5th MDS
**1992** Spot checks introduced to eliminate the use of 'porters' to aid elite runners
**1995** 213 competitors take part in the 10th MDS; first race supported by Doctrotter
**1997** Lahcen Ahansal, a local carpenter, wins the MDS for the first time on his fifth attempt
**2000** Race organizers publish a photo book to celebrate 15th anniversary of MDS. Anti-doping tests introduced in accordance with IAF principles
**2005** 766 competitors take part in the 20th MDS
**2007** A competitor (Bernard Julé) dies the morning after completing the 70km stage. Lahcen Ahansal wins the MDS for an incredible tenth time

# COMRADES
## MARATHON

THE COMRADES MARATHON is the world's largest ultra-marathon. It was first run in 1921, and its legacy is intertwined into the fabric of South Africa. The race has appeal on many dimensions and its own constitution declares the event is '*A celebration of mankind's spirit over adversity*'.

The Comrades was originally conceived by Vic Clapham. Clapham's objective was to organize a race in memory of the South African soldiers who had lost their lives in the Great War. He and many of his comrades had endured a 2,700km route march during the war and Clapham wanted to create a race that would similarly 'test the spirit'. Clapham's own spirit was tested when his first two requests for permission were denied on the basis that authorities felt a 90km race to be beyond the reasonable endurance of most people. To Clapham, that was almost certainly the point.

The race course alternates direction each year. The races are categorized as 'up' and 'down' runs, with a special medal for 'rookies' who complete both back-to-back. Until competitors have completed both, they are not considered to be true 'Comraders'. Somewhat surprisingly given the differences in ascent and descent, the race records in both directions are similar.

Today the course terrain comprises primarily tarmac road. In many places, competitors' senses are assailed by the tempting smell of *braiis*, the South African BBQ, and loud rock music. Supportive spectators party the day away, whilst watching the slightly insane push themselves to the limit.

The party atmosphere is deceptive: Comrades is a tough race. The run is characterized by the 'big five' hills: Cowies Hill, Field's Hill, Botha's Hill, Inchanga, and finally, the notorious Polly Shortts.

The event is particularly rich in history and tradition. Each year, medals are awarded on the basis of five classifications, including one to commemorate Bill Cowan's original winning time and one to honour the race founder. A wall of honour overlooks the Valley of a Thousand Hills, which is built with commemorative bricks that have been purchased by past competitors.

**OPPOSITE** Runners of all abilities attempt to break the strict 12-hour time barrier.

**BELOW** Watching the race is as much a national passion as running in the event.

And those dedicated runners who have completed 10 races are presented with their own race numbers, set against a green background.

Perhaps the most dramatic moment in the Comrades each year is when the selected official or celebrity stands on the finish line with his or her back to the oncoming runners and fires the cut-off gun to formally close the race. Any competitor who has not completed the race by that moment, regardless of how agonizingly close he or she may be to the finish line, is not recognized as an 'official finisher'.

The South African nation stops for a day each year to watch and celebrate the Comrades Marathon. There is live TV and radio coverage from start to finish, which is in excess of 13 hours. Yet despite the massive growth in the field, from 34 to a peak of 23,000 runners in 2000, the race remains true to its founding principles.

## KEY DATA

**RACE** Comrades Marathon
**LOCATION** Durban/Pietermaritzburg (Kwazulu-Natal, South Africa)
**DISTANCE** 90km (56 miles), single stage
**DATE** June
**TOTAL ASCENT** 1,778m (5,835ft); 'up' run
**TOTAL DESCENT** 1,173m (3,850ft); 'up' run
**KEY CHARACTERISTICS** Historic ultra-marathon on road with a strict 12-hour time limit
**RACE RECORDS** Down Hill: Male 5:24, Female 5:54 / Up Hill: Male 5:25, Female 6:09
**FIELD (APPROX)** 11,000
**CLIMATE** 30°C (86°F)
**FINISHERS** 80% of starters
**RACE DIRECTOR** Renee Smith
**EMAIL** info@comrades.com
**WEB** www.comrades.com

# LE GRAND RAID
## DE LA RÉUNION

THE REMOTE volcanic island of Réunion, situated in the Indian Ocean 220km south-west of Mauritius, is part of France. What it lacks in sun-kissed beaches it makes up for in its rugged terrain of jungles, lava desert, rain forest and high mountainous plateaus. Réunion is an adventure racer's paradise. Its extreme isolation serves only to enhance its appeal, as does its crowning glory — one of the world's most active volcanoes.

The Grand Raid, on Réunion Island, is a 143km traverse, the length of the island 'diagonally' from southeast to northwest, which crosses five major passes. The Grand Raid's tag-line *La Diagonale des Fous* literally translates as 'The Diagonal of the Insane' (or 'The Cross-Country for Crazies'), which aptly captures the extreme nature of the race. The average incline on the route is 10 per cent but sections

**BELOW** Crossing the hardened molten lava near the active 'Piton de la Fournaise' volcano rim.

reach up to 30 per cent gradients. The course contains a total of 8,000m ascent and descent. Undulating is something this course is not and the 63-hour cut-off time limit is challenging.

The race commences with a harsh initiation at 1am. Competitors soon reach an extremely steep 2,300m ascent, first through sugar cane fields and then through rain forest leading up to the rim of the volcano. As competitors emerge from the trees, they are rewarded with the view of an entirely alien environment. It is shaped by centuries of flow of molten lava. An eruption from the bubbling crater of 'The Furnance' (Piton de la Fournaise) is not impossible. While the other volcanoes on the island are inactive, the Piton de la Fournaise has had 125 recorded eruptions in the last century alone. The last major eruption occurred as recently as April 2007, when sprays of magma reached 200m high and flowed across the main coast road and into the sea.

At the 37km mark is the summit of Oratoire St Thérèse, the highest point on the course (2,411m). However, there are still two further peaks above 2,000m, including the top of Col du Taïbit (2,080m), and some 1,500m of descent from that high point.

There are frequent checkpoints along the course and two major aid stations (at Cilaos and Riviere des Galets) that provide hot food and sleeping facilities.

The journey from Cape Malicious to Saint Denis is arduous. The scenery is stunning, but the remote and unfamiliar environment is disarming. Moreover, the course profile is alarming with its endless, steep ascents and matching steep descents through hostile and unknown terrain. Yet the magic of this island paradise is powerful. It leaves any visitor with a real sense of wonder at what nature can achieve with a volcano and two million years.

## KEY DATA

RACE Le Grand Raid de La Réunion
LOCATION Réunion Island (France)
DISTANCE 143km (89 miles), single stage
DATE October
TOTAL ASCENT 8,000m (26,250ft)
TOTAL DESCENT 8,000m (26,250ft)
KEY CHARACTERISTICS Semi-self sufficiency mountain race on remote island of Réunion that encompasses various terrains and an active volcano
RACE RECORDS Male: 20:39, Female: 26:33
FIELD (APPROX) 2000
CLIMATE Day: 30°C (86°F), humid; Night: 0°C (32°F)
FINISHERS 65% of starters
RACE DIRECTOR Robert Chicaud
EMAIL info@grandraid-reunion.com
WEB www.grandraid-reunion.com

ABOVE The race commences at 1am for the field of 2,000 runners.

# 'The more restricted our society and work become, the more necessary it will be to find some outlet for this craving for freedom.'

**Sir Roger Bannister**

# TRANS **333**

**OPPOSITE** Great portions of the race are spent in solitude as the small number of competitors spread out over 50km apart.

**BELOW** The Trans 333 is the longest, single-stage desert race in the world.

THE TRANS 333 is a foot race that takes place in a different host country each year. In the last nine years, it has been held in Mauritania, Tunisia, India and Niger. The 2006 race was hosted in the Ténéré Desert, Niger, and the 2007 event will be held in Oman. Wherever the race is held, there will be local interest, as people come to see those who choose to run across the desert – a desert that they themselves venture into only when absolutely necessary.

The Trans 333 is the longest, single-stage desert race in the world. Participants require cast-iron will and sheer physical strength to complete this vast distance, in challenging conditions.

The extraordinarily demanding event attracts a very small field, which has a bearing on the level of support available. Competitors must rely on fellow participants in the field of 20, which spreads over 50km of desert.

Great portions of the race are covered in solitude. The detachment of running (or shuffling) through the desert, at night, with nothing but a narrow cone of light from a head torch to provide comfort, is an isolating experience. The hallucinogenic effect of severe fatigue, and associated disorientation, can lead to real and dangerous problems. Among other things, the route is not marked on the ground. Instead, the night before the race starts, the organizers issue each runner with a road book, which contains a series of way points. Runners must carefully programme their GPS devices, which will be their only reference to guide them from checkpoint to checkpoint.

Logistical support is also sparse. Checkpoints are spaced at roughly 22km intervals. Race organizers deliver 'drop bags', containing runners' spare clothing and food at selected checkpoints. There are long periods between: the maximum time permitted to complete the course is 108 hours.

Although the Trans 333 is not a self-sufficiency race as such, competitors must carry mandatory safety equipment, food and approximately 3 litres of water between checkpoints. With very little relief and virtually no landmarks to help gauge pace, progress is often significantly slower than expected; checkpoints seem further apart than they should be, which has an effect on the mind. More importantly, it may also have a significant bearing on water management. Running out of water in the heat of the day is extremely serious.

Many ultra-races test athletes' physical endurance and mental willpower. None pushes competitors to the limit of the Trans 333. The four-and-a-half day event has tough cut-off times, so anything more than a short cat-nap en route simply is not an option. The endless fatigue, the monotonous isolation of a small field in a vast desert and a course of 333km, make this event one of greatest individual challenges left to the modern-day adventurer.

## KEY DATA

**RACE** Trans 333
**LOCATION** Desert location (host country changes each year)
**DISTANCE** 333km (206 miles), single stage
**DATE** November
**TOTAL ASCENT** Course varies each year
**TOTAL DESCENT** Course varies each year
**KEY CHARACTERISTICS** World's longest single stage desert race
**RACE RECORDS** Course varies each year
**FIELD (APPROX)** 20
**CLIMATE** Day: 30–35°C (86–95°F); Night: 14°C (57°F)
**FINISHERS** 75–80% of starters
**RACE DIRECTOR** Alain Gestin
**EMAIL** alain.gestin4@wanadoo.fr
**WEB** www.extreme-runner.com

# 'It is not because things are difficult that we do not dare, it is because we do not dare that things are difficult.'
**Seneca (Roman philosopher, mid-1st century AD)**

3

NORTH AMERICA

# BADWATER
## ULTRAMARATHON

THE LEGENDARY BADWATER ULTRAMARATHON is run in the hostile environs of California's Death Valley. Death Valley's own tourism authority describes the region as the '*driest, hottest and lowest*' part of North America. The description may not be enticing to the average tourist, but for those seeking out new frontiers in extreme running it has real appeal.

The race's namesake is Badwater Basin, a geological basin that marks the single lowest point in the Western Hemisphere, with an elevation of 86m below sea level. It boasts a small spring-fed pool of water, which is made undrinkable by accumulated salt deposits, hence the name Badwater. It is that small pool of undrinkable water that marks the start of the 217km Badwater Ultramarathon. There is no little irony in starting an endurance race, in which hydration and management of fluid intake is the single most important factor, at an undrinkable water source.

The invitation-only event brings together a field of 90-odd of the world's toughest athletes, who are required to run virtually non-stop from Death Valley to Mt. Whitney. The course takes runners over three mountain ranges for a total of 3,962m of cumulative vertical ascent and 1,433m of cumulative descent. The finish line is at the Mt. Whitney Portals, at 2,533m, which are the trailhead to the Mt. Whitney summit, the highest point in the contiguous United States.

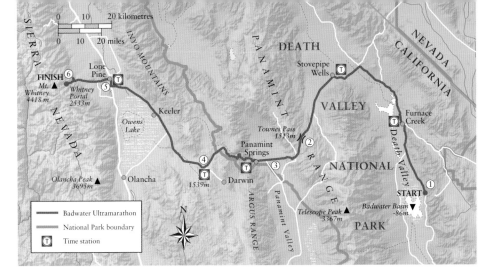

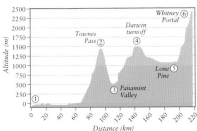

## 'Hottest, Driest, Lowest…
## A place of legend and a
## place of trial. Death Valley.'
**Death Valley National Park Service website**

This race does not wear its moniker of the 'Toughest Footrace on Earth' lightly. It takes participants (runners and crew) through some of the most hostile territory on earth. The asphalt highway might be perceived by off-road runners to be a luxury and a saviour. In reality, that searing black ribbon, weaving its way through the valley, traps the shimmering heat in this furnace-like bowl. Temperatures reach in excess of 55° Celsius). A clue is in the names of the towns along the route, which include Devils Cornfield, Furnace Creek and Stovepipe Wells. The sleepy town of Lone Pine, which is near the base of Mount Whitney, has an almost oasis-sounding name in contrast. If the geography and heat were not enough, race organizers impose a 60-hour limit in which runners must reach the finish line, located in the cool pine glades high up Mount Whitney.

In distance terms, the Badwater Ultramarathon extends just beyond five, consecutive, non-stop marathons. In practice, it boils (literally) down to five major sections: the pre-race preparation; the initial and shocking plunge into the midday heat of the Death Valley's cauldron; the long, slow and relentless crawl out of the furnace from

**OPPOSITE** The long, straight road across Panamint Valley.

**ABOVE** Understated park entrance sign to the unique environs of Death Valley.

IN 1977, AL ARNOLD and his support crew proved that running from the most hellish place on earth to the tallest mountain in the contiguous United States was physically possible. It took the 49-year-old Arnold 84 hours to complete the distance and it was his third attempt in four years. Four years later, Jay Birmingham upped the ante with a faster time, but it would be 1987 before four athletes would attempt the course in a head-to-head battle. And so the annual

Badwater Ultramarathon was born.

A true 'challenge of the champions', this legendary foot race pits up to 90 of the world's toughest athletes against one another and the elements. Covering 135 miles (217km) non-stop from Death Valley to Mt. Whitney, CA in temperatures up to 130°F (55°C), it is the most demanding and extreme running race offered anywhere on the planet.

The race starts from Badwater in Death Valley, the lowest point in the

Western Hemisphere, and finishes at Mt. Whitney Portal, the trailhead to the highest point in the contiguous United States, Mt Witney summit. The race takes competitors through places or landmarks with names like Mushroom Rock, Furnace Creek, Salt Creek, Devil's Cornfield, Devil's Golf Course, Stovepipe Wells, Keeler and Lone Pine.

**Chris Kostman**
CHIEF ADVENTURE OFFICER AND
RACE DIRECTOR

**ABOVE** Support crews travel alongside runners for every kilometre of the course. Vehicles need to be air-conditioned and carry up to 100 litres of water.

Stovepipe Wells over to Panamint Valley; the ascent from Panamint Springs through the Argus Range and across Owens Valley; and, finally, the lonely trek out of Lone Pine to climb up and up to the heady (and surprisingly cool) Mount Whitney Portals. Each section presents unique and startling challenges. Each participant must find the personal strength and strategy to overcome all of those challenges in order to successfully conquer this extraordinary event.

## The Pre-event – Getting To The Start Line

It goes without saying that this race requires intense training and preparation. Being an invitation-only event, potential runners must provide a 'running resumé' to persuade the event organizers that they fall into the category of elite sportspeople who are capable of even attempting this challenge.

Badwater is a test of strategy and the preparation and implementation of that strategy begins well before the race start. Participants need to build up running fitness to a level that will sustain them through five back-to-back marathons. They also need to prepare for the heat. Race veterans favour using saunas to accustom the body to the heat. A former Badwater medical director and race veteran, Dr. Lisa Bliss, explains that '*When you heat-acclimate your body it learns to sweat sooner, sweat more, and how to sweat with less sodium loss. You have to learn how to process more fluid, because if someone was to drink the amount we consume in the desert they would be sick. I was able to drink two litres of water every half hour at Badwater with no problems.*'

The nearest international airports to Death Valley are Las Vegas and Los Angeles. From Las Vegas, it is a 250km drive in an almost straight line. There is virtually no way to obtain any serious provisions once in the Valley, so everything must be planned in painstaking detail before leaving the city (usually Las Vegas). Even bottled water and ice – a basic requirement for survival in the desert – is difficult to restock during the event.

Every runner needs a crew (minimum of two people) and a vehicle. The vehicle needs to be big and air-conditioned. For safety reasons, the organizers require that the vehicles be clearly marked with the runner's name and race number at the sides and rear, along with a 'Caution: Runners on Road' sign. It needs to be loaded with the runner and crew's gear, food and supplies, all necessary race equipment and as much ice and water as the vehicle can carry. Multiple coolers need to be stacked in the vehicle for drinking water, cooling water, water for mixing energy drinks and food and water for cleaning the salt, dust, blood and sand from the runner's face and eyes.

It is impossible to pack too much water. The toughest battle for the crew throughout the race will be keeping the runner cool. Various methods are favoured by race veterans, including plunging the whole body into a roadside ice bath set up in a giant, body-sized cooler.

**ABOVE** A family affair at Furnace Creek.

**BOTTOM** Three runners, in typical all-white attire, head out from the start.

The truth is that the human body is not designed to run in 55°C temperatures. By the time the atmosphere reaches 35°C, the body will lose its capacity to release heat into the air. Activity accelerates the process. The maximum core temperature measured in a conscious long-distance runner has been 41°C degrees. At 42.7°C body temperature, the runner will collapse. At that stage, the body has begun to pump blood out to the body's outermost layers in an effort to radiate heat. In the meantime, the internal organs are thus deprived of their blood supply, and the thermoregulatory system starts to shut down. The first physical sign of this process is when, despite the searing heat and apparent full hydration, the body simply ceases to sweat. From that stage, if the body goes untreated, serious inflammation and cell damage may ensue and affect the central nervous system. At that point, death can be sudden.

The importance of water (and the need continually to stay cool) cannot be over-estimated. But this is a long event — up to 60 hours — so careful food planning is also critical. Runners usually subsist mainly on liquid supplements, as well as some solid foods, during the event. It is not unusual for a runner to consume up to 120 calories every 20–30 minutes in Death Valley. Individual runners know what

**BELOW** Scott Jurek, race record holder, approaching Lone Pine, with Mt Whitney towering in the background.

**OPPOSITE** Traditional pre-start photo at Badwater Basin, the lowest point in the Western Hemisphere.

they like most to eat. Individual runners know what their body can and cannot tolerate in extreme conditions and during sustained periods of physical exertion. That said, the particular conditions during the Badwater Ultramarathon may require runners to revise their usual liquid supplement 'mix' and be nimble and ready to make changes to tried and tested habits.

Equally important as water, food and the vehicle, is the runner's crew. No-one could run, or undertake any exercise, in Death Valley conditions in July without considerable support and assistance. The race rules stipulate a minimum of two. The rules also stipulate a maximum of six (after one competitor in 2005 engaged the services of no less than 43 crew members). Crews must work non-stop to ensure the runner remains hydrated and race-fit to the finish line. The tasks necessary to meet those goals are multiple. The crew members must take care of the runner (cooling, water and food provision), mix drinks and solutions, manage the support vehicle (and all its contents), replenish supplies en route, offer psychological and moral support, and provide physical and medical monitoring and aid as required (including heat treatment, blister management, massage and constantly looking out for signs of slurred speech, dizziness, lack of sweat or urination).

## KEY DATA

**RACE** Badwater Ultramarathon
**LOCATION** Death Valley (California, USA)
**DISTANCE** 217km (135 miles), single stage
**DATE** Mid–Late July
**TOTAL ASCENT** 3,962m (13,000ft)
**TOTAL DESCENT** 1,433m (4,700ft)
**KEY CHARACTERISTICS** Start in Badwater Basin (-85m), lowest point in USA, finish in Whitney Portal (2,533m) on highest mountain in contiguous USA.
**RACE RECORDS** Male: 24:36, Female: 27:56
**FIELD (APPROX)** Limited to 90 (invitation only)
**CLIMATE** Up to 55°C (130°F), dry
**FINISHERS** 75–80% of starters
**RACE DIRECTOR** Chris Kostman
**EMAIL** outthere@adventurecorps.com
**WEB** www.badwater.com

Without a reliable and experienced support crew, the race can turn to disaster very quickly. As the double race winner and record holder, Scott Jurek says, '*There are no aid stations out there, so your crew is your lifeline.*'

# Death Valley's Cauldron

The Badwater Ultramarathon is run in North America's midsummer, in the searing heat of July. Nothing can prepare participants for the extraordinary force of heat that is contained within the Death Valley atmosphere. There are unique geographical factors that combine to create exceptional conditions. As a general climatic rule, temperatures are higher in places where altitude is lowest. Death Valley is indeed low: at over 85m below sea level, it is the seventh lowest place in the world. In addition to that, a series of high mountain ranges encircle the valley, which causes it to radiate extreme amounts of heat. The combination generates some of

the highest temperatures on earth. The highest temperature in the United States on record is 56.7°C. It was recorded at Furnace Creek in mid-July and was a world record at the time. (Since then, only the Libyan Sahara has recorded a higher temperature at 57.8°C.) In addition, the ground temperature in Death Valley can reach up to 40 per cent higher than the surrounding air temperature.

Participants are strongly recommended to spend three to four days at Furnace Creek to acclimatize prior to the start of the event. Furnace Creek has a surprising array of recreational activities, including a golf course and swimming pool. Furnace Creek golf course is watered continuously in summer in an effort to preserve the greens and is a genuine golf course, as opposed to the nearby 'Devil's Golf Course'. The swimming pool is fed by a natural underground, thermal spring. Consequently, it is heated and provides no relief whatsoever to the overwhelming heat (but does aid acclimatization).

The race starts with an early morning drive back up the valley to Badwater. Runners set off in three waves staged at two hour intervals at 6am, 8am and 10am. The runners' start times are carefully calculated to ensure that everyone is forced to endure the full force of the midday heat in the middle of the valley. It is

# 'It was inevitable that the new breed of Ultramarathoners looking for a unique challenge would come across this geographical and meteorological anomaly and embrace it.'

**Richard Benyo, *The Death Valley 300: Near-Death and Redemption on the World's Toughest Endurance Course* (1991)**

a surreal sight seeing 90 runners clothed in white from top to toe emerging from the shimmering roadside heat. They make their way – many walking as they confront the reality of the heat for the first time – the 28km from Badwater back to Furnace Creek.

The next 39km from Furnace Creek to Stovepipe Wells comprise the hottest part of the course. It is almost impossible to convey just how hot it becomes in this brutal corner of the world. It is simply too hot and too dry for any moisture to last more than a few minutes (or even seconds). Yet 90 extraordinary human beings – whose bodies consist of 60 per cent water – are out in those conditions running for hours and hours on end.

In normal circumstances, the human body would generate sweat to cool itself down. In Death Valley, it is simply too hot for the body to generate enough sweat to be effective; what is generated soon evaporates in the heat and dryness and thus has no impact. As a substitute, runners must rely on their crew to douse them with icy cold water, either from spray bottles or heavily soaked towels. Within minutes of being saturated with icy cold water, the runner will find his or her clothes and towels have dried rigid and stiff around them. And the dousing process begins over again, continually through the day.

The elite runners will reach Stovepipe Wells, the 67.4km mark, sometime before dusk. The rest of the field will arrive anytime between early evening and midnight.

**BELOW** The air temperature can reach 55°C but the ground temperature, radiating off the road, can be up to 40 per cent higher again.

Paradoxically, the setting of the sun in the evening brings runners no respite from the heat. The anticipated relief of the impending cool night air becomes palpable by the late afternoon. Twelve hours is a long time to maintain any form of movement in temperatures of 55°C in the glaring sun. Yet the refreshingly cool night simply never descends. Instead, the sun goes down and leaves in its wake a thick and heavy night air, which closes oppressively around everything within its reach. It seems to prevent the retained heat from the day from escaping. It just sits in the air and emanates from the dark road underfoot. In July, overnight lows may dip only into the 32°–38°C range.

The swimming pool at Stovepipe Wells is the Badwater competitor's elixir of life. It is, unlike the pool at Furnace Creek, cool and refreshing. It is also very difficult to leave. A quiet bathe late on the first day gives runners a few minutes to reflect on the preceding hours, and those that are to follow. But beware, the time to reflect may prove fatal; Stovepipe Wells is a common drop-out point in the race.

## Out of the Furnace from Stovepipe Wells

Stovepipe Wells marks the end of Death Valley, and the beginning of the climb up the foothills that lead over to the neighbouring Panamint Valley. The monotony of the Death Valley flat comes to an abrupt end. There is a 27km ascent up to Townes Pass at 1,513m. The final 8km are the steepest with just under 10 per cent gradient. Also, there are multiple (heartbreaking) false summits before the pass. From the top of the pass, it is a 22km descent into Panamint Springs and the halfway point in the race. Runners must be careful to prevent feet from blistering on the descent. At the bottom of Townes Pass on the Panamint Valley side is a long, mostly straight, causeway that carves a line through a vast and dry salt bed. Highway 190 draws a long, hard black line through the pale and dusty dry lake bed that marks Panamint Valley.

As Dean Karnazes, the 2004 race winner, points out '*Badwater is about overcoming low points and persevering.*' At Panamint Springs, the race organizers provide bunk beds in a communal cabin. Competitors are able to borrow a few hours to power nap and refresh for the next leg. It is difficult to identify whether it is the bed, the comfortable sleep, the food, the shower, or simply the satisfaction of reaching the halfway point, but Panamint Springs is a real milestone for runners.

## Ascent from Panamint Springs

From the tiny township (that prospers from the annual influx of Badwater runners and crew), the route ascends again for 28.6km to Darwin Turnoff through the Argus Range. The climb from 600m to 1,539m is arduous, but the heat begins to lift ever

so slightly as the valleys are left behind. Darwin Turnoff marks the 145km mark. The worst is over, perhaps.

For many competitors, this is the onset of their second night running and brings potentially new demons. The night before the race starts, runners are provided with basic desert safety information, which includes an introduction to the potentially dangerous insects and reptiles that make this inhospitable environment their home. As night falls, exhaustion and monotony has a peculiar way of transforming every crack in the road into a venomous snake, and every stick or bug into a scorpion.

From Darwin Turnoff, the route is calm and flat along the edge of the dry Owens Lake for approximately 51.8km to Lone Pine. The searing heat of the previous day is a thing of the past. The promise of Mount Whitney, and the finish line, lies in sight as the Sierra Nevada mountain range comes into distant view at dawn. The road continues parallel to the range up to the township of Lone Pine. This small, wild west town is the staging post to climb Mt. Whitney or the southern terminus of the John Muir Trail.

Lone Pine is the place where runners spend the night at the end of the race. The hotel is booked, the bed is ready and the shower is full of fresh, flowing water. Cruelly, after a whistle-stop tour to take all this in and to refuel (and perhaps take a quick nap if absolutely necessary), runners are forced to rouse themselves one last time and leave it all behind to set foot back out on the road. It can be a difficult and lonely step to take – but the end is near.

**BELOW LEFT** Clothing and towels dry stiff within minutes of being soaked in icy water.

**BELOW RIGHT** 2004 race winner Dean Karnazes takes an 'ice bath' to lower his core body temperature.

## The Final Push

The final 19km take runners from Lone Pine up a 1,450m ascent to the Mt Whitney Portals. It is a beautiful, scenic site and the starting point for summits of Mt Whitney and many other treks in the area. It is accessed by a steep, rocky, narrow and uneven track that is built for 4x4 vehicles rather than blistered and bruised feet. At this stage in the race, it takes most runners between 5 and 8 hours to reach the Portals.

The Mount Whitney foothills are the Alabama Hills, site of the great 1950s western movies. It is dusty and rugged and the place where the true pioneer spirit needs to kick in.

Slowly, the vegetation increases as the road climbs up the hills. Dusty stations and tourist cottages give way to heavy foliages. The terrain can become testing on the one-lane dirt road.

The higher the road climbs, the taller the pine trees tower above and the deeper the water-fed canyons flow. Eventually, after seemingly endless twists and turns, are signs marked 'Campsites 39–44', 'Family Campsites', and then the car park 'Overflow'. From the 'Overflow' sign it is 200m to the finish line.

In true Badwater tradition, runners and crew cross the finish line together. It is very much a shared race and it is only right to share the prize of successful completion. The race director is there to shake hands with the finisher and

**ABOVE** Tackling the 10 per cent gradient climb up to the top of Townes Pass (1,513m).

ABOVE RIGHT In true Badwater
tradition, runners and support
crew cross the finish line
together.

present him or her with a race medal and the coveted Badwater belt buckle – if the finishing time is 48 hours or under – or a t-shirt if 60 hours and under.

Almost invariably, despite making their own way 217km across some of the most hostile and inhospitable conditions on earth, runners need their crew to assist them back to the support vehicle after crossing the finish line. The mental and physical fortitude that holds these individuals together through this extraordinary difficult trial seems to stretch as far as the finishing tape and not beyond. From there, it is a bumpy but satisfying drive back down to that awaiting shower, meal and – most critically – bed.

# 'You must simply respect the Valley so that it lets you pass.'
**Marshall Ulrich, 4 time race winner and 13 time finisher**

**1973** Paxton Beale and Ken Crutchlow complete a 240km (150 mile) relay run from Badwater to the top of Mount Whitney

**1977** Al Arnold becomes the first person to run the same route 'solo' in 84 hours – effectively giving birth to the Badwater Ultramarathon

**1981** Jay Birmingham becomes second finisher in a time of 75hrs 34mns

**1987** Ken Crutchlow organizes the first actual head-to-head race (an America versus UK team event)

**1988** Eight runners compete in the first commercially sponsored race (only four finish).

**1989** Tom Crawford and Richard Benyo complete the first ever Badwater 'double' (Badwater to Mt. Whitney return) in 126 hrs & 170 hrs respectively

**1990** The Forest Service forces the race to stop at the Mt. Whitney Portals, thereby creating the 217km (135 mile) course used today.

**1996** The time limit to be awarded the coveted Badwater belt buckle is set at 48 hours (overall race finish cut-off is 60 hours)

**1999** Marshall Ulrich becomes the first person to complete original Badwater course 'unassisted' in 77hrs 46mns (pulling a two-wheeled cart initially loaded up with 102kg, including 77kg of water)

**2002** Marshall Ulrich and Jack Denness are first runners to successfully finish 10 Badwater Ultramarathons

**2002** Pamela Reed becomes first ever female outright winner in a time of 27:56:47 (she repeats the achievement in 2003)

**2005** Scott Jurek, aged 31, becomes the youngest winner and sets a new course record of 24:36:08 (he returns to win again in 2006)

**BELOW** A road-side rest and meal during the night.

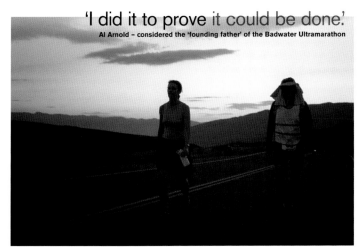

# 'I did it to prove it could be done.'
### Al Arnold – considered the 'founding father' of the Badwater Ultramarathon

**LEFT** Night temperatures remain high as the unique climate prevents the retained day heat from escaping.

# PIKES PEAK
# **MARATHON**

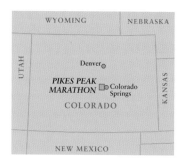

THE PIKES PEAK MARATHON is a 21km ascent from Manitou Springs at 1,920m to the summit of Pikes Peak at 4,302m and then a 21km descent back down again. The average gradient is 11% but much of the course is considerably steeper. The race is one of the older modern adventure foot races, having started in 1956.

Pikes Peak is itself a popular destination for travellers. There is even a gift shop and visitors centre at the summit. There is also a train that runs from Manitou Springs to the summit year round and a vehicle access road. The local tourist board claims that Pikes Peak is *'the most visited mountain in North America and the second most visited mountain in the world behind Japan's Mount Fuji'.*

**BELOW** View towards the spectacular 'cirque' at 4,050m and 2.25km from the summit.

Nonetheless, the general accessibility of the summit due to modern transport options does nothing to detract from the difficulty of the Pikes Peak Marathon. Although the average incline is 11 per cent, near the summit the incline increases to a breathtaking 20 per cent. At 3,000m, still 1,000m from the summit, competitors will begin to feel the effects of the altitude and that, combined with an increasingly steep route, is exhausting. It is at this stage that the notoriously misleading signpost declaring the start of 'The 16 Stairs' to the summit comes into view. The 16 'stairs' are in fact 16 long and punishing 'switch backs' to the peak.

The final few kilometres are above the tree line and the route may require some rock climbing in addition to track running. The falling oxygen pressure merely exacerbates the ordeal. These are not conditions where runners, or anyone, should dwell for longer than necessary. Upon reaching the summit, Matt Carpenter (seven-time race winner) advises competitors to: '...*grab some food and water and get out of there. Keep a steady pace and try to descend as quickly as you can. There is more food, water and most importantly, air down below.*'

As any hill runner will testify, the descent is no time for relaxation. Steep downhill descents are incredibly difficult on the legs and knees in particular. Injuries are common. And even the increasing oxygen does little to ease the muscle pain that is the result of an endless and agonizing climb, followed by a rapid, high impact descent.

Pikes Peak is a daunting race that adds an additional psychological twist: once on the trail, the only way off is either up or down under one's own steam. One way or another, runners must make it to the summit and, if they choose to do so, turn around and make it back down again to the finish line.

**ABOVE** East face – the race course side – of Pikes Peak, from the Garden of the Gods Park in Colorado Springs.

## KEY DATA

**RACE** Pikes Peak Marathon
**LOCATION** Manitou Springs (Colorado, USA)
**DISTANCE** 42km (26.2 miles), single stage
**DATE** August
**TOTAL ASCENT** 2,381m (7,800ft)
**TOTAL DESCENT** 2,366m (7,700ft)
**KEY CHARACTERISTICS** An out and back mountain race up Pikes Peak
**RACE RECORDS** Male 3:16, Female, 4:15
**FIELD (APPROX)** 800
**CLIMATE** Start: 15–21°C (60-70°F), Summit: 2–12°C (35-55°F)
**FINISHERS** 85% of starters
**RACE DIRECTOR** Ron Ilgen (President)
**EMAIL** raceinfo@pikespeakmarathon.org
**WEB** www.pikespeakmarathon.org

# WASATCH FRONT
# 100 MILER

'The magic
is in the man,
not the 100
miles.'
**Bill Bowerman**

THE WASATCH FRONT 100 MILER is one of the oldest and toughest 100-mile races in the USA. It is also the final race in the series of four 100 Milers that make up the classic ultra-running 'Grand Slam', which must be completed in a single year. The Grand Slam also includes: Western States Endurance Run (Sierra Nevada, California – June); Vermont 100 Mile Endurance Run

(West Windsor, Vermont – July); and Leadville Trail 100 Ultra-marathon (Leadville, Colorado – August), also known as 'The Race Across the Sky' as the trail ranges in elevation between 2,800–3,800m. The commemorative Eagle Trophy is awarded to successful 'Grand Slammers' at the award ceremony for the Wasatch 100.

The Wasatch 100 takes place in September and competitors must complete the scenic, but mountainous, route between Layton and The Homestead in Midway, Utah in 36 hours.

The race contains two major climbs; the 1,220m grunt up 'Chinscraper' commencing after only 7km, and Catherine's Pass (3,121m) the highest point on the course, at Mile 78. The altitude remains relatively constant, between 8–9,000 feet, throughout the route. The total cumulative ascent is 8,190m – almost the height of Mt Everest. This is matched by a similar amount of rocky descent, which is brutal and punishing.

During the day, the heat exceeds 35°C (100 °F). Temperatures plummet at night and in the high altitude, sometimes to freezing. In addition, rain is a distinct possibility. Runners are usually unsupported and forced to rely on the eight aid-stations, five of which are designated 'bag-drops'. Access to personally tailored nutrition and alternative clothing is

**BELOW** An early morning start allows runners to make good progress in cooler temperatures.

available at the 'bag drops', but this is severely limited when compared with the assistance available to any competitor supported by crew.

As with all of the Grand Slam events, the Wasatch 100 course follows Forestry Service Trails. A pre-requisite for entry to the race is a day's voluntary work in the forests to build new trails and/or restore the existing trails. International competitors are expected to conform to the spirit of this regulation and undertake voluntary work with their nation's equivalent of the American Forestry Service.

Athletes and crew that step up to the challenge of the Wasatch 100 are rewarded with an awe-inspiring experience. By day, the rolling views over the Wasatch Mountains are spectacular whilst at night the sky is resplendent with stars. The dichotomy of the race is neatly summed up in its slogan: *'One Hundred Miles of Heaven and Hell'*. Whether completing the race as a stand-alone event, or the final quartet of the Grand Slam, the Wasatch 100 is the standard for other 100-milers and is truly an exceptional feat of endurance.

## KEY DATA

**RACE** Wasatch 100 Miler
**LOCATION** Kaysville (Utah, USA)
**DISTANCE** 160km (100 miles), single stage
**DATE** September
**TOTAL ASCENT** 8,190m (26,882ft)
**TOTAL DESCENT** 7,960m (26,131ft)
**KEY CHARACTERISTICS** One of the oldest and toughest 100 milers. Final race in the American 'Grand Slam of Ultrarunning' series
**RACE RECORDS** Male 19:43, Female 22:27
**FIELD (APPROX)** 225
**CLIMATE** -4°C to 30°C (25°F to 85°F)
**FINISHERS** 65–70% of starters
**RACE DIRECTOR** John Grobben
**EMAIL** info@wasatch100.com
**WEB** www.wasatch100.com

BELOW The total cumulative ascent over the Wasatch 100 course is 8,190m.

# YUKON
# **ARCTIC ULTRA**

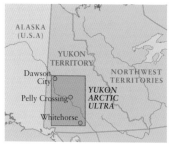

**ABOVE** Participants in the 300 mile race will take at least five-and-a-half days to complete the event.

THE YUKON ARCTIC ULTRA is more a concurrent series of races than a single event. Originally offered at two distances – 100 and 300 miles (160 and 480km) respectively – the options have grown to include the classic marathon distance as well as the mind-blowing 460-mile (740-km) race. In addition to the original disciplines, of running and mountain biking, the organisers have added cross-country skiing and skijoring. The race coincides with the Yukon Quest Trail, the world's toughest Sled Dog Race, and follows much of the same route.

The majority of the various foot races are run along the frozen waters of the Yukon and Takhini rivers. As described by the event organizers, *'high cut banks indicate areas of strong current, deep water and weak ice. The trail stays always on the shallow side of the river, where the ice is stronger and the current slow'.* Clearly a little local knowledge provides a clear advantage and it is no surprise that the elite of these fields include many Yukon runners. For others, race organizers provide a cold-weather survival course two days before the race.

# 'This is the law of the Yukon, that only the Strong shall thrive; That surely the Weak shall perish, and only the Fit survive.'

**Robert W Service (Scottish/Canadian Poet)**

The marathon ends at Sir North Ranch near Takhini Hot Springs, but this is just the first checkpoint for the ultra-run competitors. From that point, the trail is accessible only by snowmobile, and competitors must be able to survive unassisted for 24 hours in temperatures as low as -45°C. Race organizers enforce a mandatory four-hour stopover rule at Takhini, in order to ensure that competitors, and their equipment, are coping with the extreme conditions.

The course climbs and descends over snow-covered trails. Competitors use man-hauled (rigid pole) pulk sleds to carry their equipment. The constant draw of the sled tugging on the waist-harness encumbers movement, particularly when trudging in soft snow. Frozen rivers and lakes offer little respite. Commonly referred to as 'overflow', there is the constant threat of breaking through the ice into the freezing water below. Water, flowing over the ice, freezes to form ridges that further serve to impede the progress of the sled.

During the event, there are well-spaced check-points, where hot and cold liquids are served. However, competitors are warned to carry as much water as possible in the intervening sections. Dehydration occurs swiftly in the cold climate and melting snow takes a long time.

The 100 mile (160km) race may be completed in one-and-half to two-and-half days but the fastest times for the 300 mile (480km) race are just under five-and-a-half days.

Whatever distance or discipline an individual chooses, the harsh environment of the Yukon will test stamina and willpower to the core. For the ultra runner, finishing will require super-human mental and physical fortitude. The reward is the sense of achievement in knowing that they have overcome, for just a few days, an environment so extreme that survival rests on continually moving forward.

**ABOVE** Competitors use a 'pulk' sled to carry their emergency food, spare clothes and survival equipment.

## KEY DATA

**RACE** Yukon Arctic Ultra

**LOCATION** Whitehorse (Yukon, Canada)

**DISTANCE** 42, 160, 480 & 736km (26.2, 100, 300 & 460 miles), single stages

**DATE** February

**TOTAL ASCENT** No official data

**TOTAL DESCENT** No official data

**KEY CHARACTERISTICS** Semi-self sufficiency race in extreme cold pulling a sled over frozen rivers and lakes

**RACE RECORDS** No official data

**FIELD (APPROX)** Up to 20 depending on event and discipline

**CLIMATE** Down to -35°C (-31°F).

**FINISHERS** 100% of starters for marathon; 50% for the longer races

**RACE DIRECTOR** Robert Pollhammer

**EMAIL** info@thegreatoutdoors.de

**WEB** www.arcticultra.de

# JUNGLE
# MARATHON

**PAGES 81/82** Looking out over the Valle de la Muerte 'Death Valley' (Atacama Crossing). **BELOW** Start of the inaugural Jungle Marathon.

THE JUNGLE MARATHON is set within the Floresta National de Tapajós, which is part of the Amazonian state of Pará, Brazil. This tropical wet forest is characterized by its warm, humid climate with year-round rainfall. It creates running conditions that are unique and incomparable to anything else. In no other environment do competitors endure souring temperatures, interminable rain and damp, a claustrophobic and stifling jungle canopy, and the constant company of carnivorous co-habitants (here even the flora has a taste for meat). The intensity is unrelenting; the jungle never sleeps and at night the rainforest cacophony of noise remains constant as the most deadly predators emerge to hunt their prey.

In the absence of some military (or possibly scientific) background and training, individuals are likely never before to have been exposed to conditions as hostile as those of the jungle. Yet participants in the Jungle Marathon not only expose themselves to that environment,

## RACE DIRECTOR OPENING

THE JUNGLE MARATHON was created to provide runners with an opportunity to compete in an extreme environment previously untrammelled by competitors – the Jungle.

The Jungle Marathon is the only ultra race on earth that poses a real possibility for participants to encounter all of the hostilities of the jungle, including snakes, jaguars, wild pigs, scorpions, steep and muddy slopes, swamps, humidity and the general survival under the rainforest canopy.

This extraordinary adventure begins with a boat journey down the Tapajós river to the Jungle Marathon base camp in Itapuama. The two days that follow are set aside for essential acclimatization and jungle survival training to prepare competitors for the conditions beyond the camp boundaries.

The 200km race itself comprises a series of stages varying in length from an intense 16km first day to the long overnight 83km stage. Runners are warned to expect

multiple water crossings, leading to risk of confronting all manner of jungle river life (including caimans, piranhas and eels), steep slippery terrain, a series of intricate, narrow winding trails, several tiny hamlets occupied by local Amazonian villagers, and noisy evenings in hammocks, surrounded by the inky dark of nightfall in the jungle.

The Jungle Marathon is a stunningly unique adventure. The risks of the environment add to the exhilaration; the expertise and dedication of the race staff (two to every competitor) ensure that participant safety and well-being is closely monitored and managed for the duration, leaving competitors to focus on getting their bodies (and their minds) through this dauntingly challenging event.

**Shirley Thompson**
RACE DIRECTOR

but they compete in an extraordinarily challenging, multi-stage endurance event within it. The heat, humidity and unique dangers of the jungle push this event to the boundaries of extreme running.

**ABOVE** A runner maintains steady footing on the Amazon jungle floor.

The Jungle Marathon is still a relatively young race, with its inaugural event in 2003. It is now maturing into one of a handful of classic extreme events on the planet. It is a multi-stage race that requires competitors to be largely self-sufficient. The race comprises a series of six separate stages, of varying distances, which take place during both daytime and through the night. The overall distance is 200km. It is shorter than some other multi-stage events, but the heat, humidity and terrain are extremely energy-sapping and the race format has been structured to take this into

'It is only in adventure that some people succeed in knowing themselves – in finding themselves.'
**André Gide**

N

Alter do Chão
**FINISH**
Pindobal

❻ Belterra
Porto Novo

AMAZON
BASIN

Aramanaí 🔼

Rio Tapajós

Maguari

TAPAJOS-
ARAPIUNA
RESERVE

Jaguarari

❺
Pedreira

Piquiatuba

Tauari 🔼
❹
Pini 🔼

**FLORESTA**

❸ **NATIONAL**
Prainha

Paraíso 🔼 **DE**

❷ **TAPAJÓS**

Dona Irene 🔼        0        10        20 kilometres
Itapuama 🔼 ❶
**START**        0        5        10 miles

account for safety reasons. There is a 100km (half distance) option for competitors wishing to complete four of the six stages (eliminating stages five (the overnight phase) and six). Between stages, competitors are accommodated in impromptu campsites situated on the banks of the Tapajós river. The river is critical to competitor health management for the duration of the race; thorough bathing and cleansing is necessary to prevent even the most minor of cuts from becoming septic. Race withdrawal for health reasons is alarmingly common in this race and the major cause is skin infection.

The inhabitants of the Amazon Jungle are either predators, prey or both. The jaguar may be an obvious candidate for the top of the indigenous food chain, but there is a multitude of other hungry hunters, including about 2.5 million species of insects. Those that concern competitors the most are usually biting ants, spiders and scorpions at ground level, and viscous wasps, hornets and other flying beasts

'By prevailing over all obstacles and distractions, one may unfailingly arrive at his chosen goal or destination.'
**Christopher Columbus**

in the air. Others, like the massive anaconda, competitors try not even to think about.

The combined sights, smells and sounds of the Amazonian jungle are like a full frontal assault. The rainforest roof creates a canopy that filters the sunlight to cast eerily mesmerizing shadows and colours that flicker about the forest floor and walls, playing tricks on the hot and tired body and mind. The canopy also locks in the thick, complex aroma of pheromones, which are constantly released into the environment by various creatures to attract either mates or prey. The interminable noise of the jungle inhabitants is inescapable; at times, the sounds are soothing and the birdsong calming, until it spills suddenly into an alarming cacophony of screeches and shrills. It is little wonder that the Jungle Marathon website warns that *'people have been known to lose it in the jungle.'*

It is an honour to be able to run in the unspoilt, virgin terrain of the jungle. It is also a privilege, and race organizers are extremely sensitive to the environmental impact that an event such as this could have on the finely balanced ecosystem, and manage it accordingly. Organizers limit the field to around 80 participants and, at

**BELOW** Cooling down in the stifling heat and extreme humidity.

ABOVE Runners are ferried to the race start on old steamers, dating from the rubber boom.

BELOW RIGHT Runners sleep in hammocks hung from wooden lattice structures.

present, the selection occurs on a 'first come, first served' basis.

The Jungle Marathon may not be everybody's idea of 'fun-running'. But it is a unique experience that tests one's mental stamina to an extraordinary extent. A momentary lapse of concentration could easily lead to disaster. The jungle is a challenging adversary that will not be beaten. But Jungle Marathon finishers prove that it can be survived, even overcome, at least for seven days.

## Arriving in the Amazon

Most competitors meet in Santarém and are driven to Alter do Chão to board river boats for the spectacular overnight journey up the Tapajós river. The jungle base camp at Itapuama, located 120km south of Santarém, is the competitors' first night in the Amazon jungle. Standard race preparation exercises are conducted at jungle base camp, including compulsory kit checks, medical checks and the introduction to the race organizers and staff.

Then there is the four-hour jungle training session from the local jungle expert, a Brazilian army instructor. The expert teaches competitors how to make themselves relatively safe in the event that they are forced to spend a night alone in the jungle. Competitors are also taught how to find their way back to civilization, and to deal with predators including snakes, spiders, scorpions, pigs and, of course, jaguars.

# 'Through the Jungle very softly flits a shadow and a sigh – He is Fear, O Little Hunter, he is Fear.'
**Rudyard Kipling**

The jaguar is the biggest cat in the America. It is reknowned for its camouflage spots and ability to climb trees. It is extremely quiet, extremely agile and extremely strong (able to penetrate a turtle shell with its jaws) and it has excellent night vision. Its effective jungle camouflage makes it extraordinarily difficult to see; but it almost certainly is nearby, watching the race unfold and the solitary participants passing clumsily through its territory.

The jungle is an unfamiliar and hostile environment, mostly because of its inhabitants.

## The Six Stages of the Jungle Marathon

Each day follows a similar format, the main difference being the distances to be covered by the competitors and the strictly observed cut-off times. After a short race briefing on the challenges of the day's course competitors are released to race to the next campsite. The route crosses swamps, rivers and creeks, climbs and descends, and features a mixture of jungle tracks, roads, beaches and riverbeds – an all-round challenge, in fact.

**ABOVE** The trail is extremely muddy and a mass of tangled tree roots and undergrowth.

### STAGE 1 – THE 'WARM-UP'

The first stage of the Jungle Marathon is a relatively short jaunt through the rainforest for a distance of 16.3 kilometres. Yet the stage cut-off time is 10 hours 30 minutes. It is during this first stage that, on average, 10 to 15 per cent of participants drop out or are withdrawn.

This warm-up is, in fact, a rapid introduction (or baptism by fire) to what it is like to run in the jungle environs. Runners must contend with an environment that is literally trying to trip them up at every opportunity. The terrain is tough and the trail is a labyrinth of tree branches and roots. Creepers weave their way across the trail, creating a series of obstacles to trip and injure tired feet.

At every turn, there are thorn-covered branches to tear at clothing and, if exposed, flesh. The combination of the heat and wet is exhausting and shocking. Sweat oozes from every pore and in the humid atmosphere it lingers on the body, quickly drenching clothing. Creek crossings are frequent and shoes and socks are quickly saturated, rubbing against feet to form blisters. The trail climbs harshly and there are difficult traverses along steep slopes, putting pressure on feet as competitors constantly fight to prevent themselves sliding down the slopes.

At all times in the jungle, hygiene is critical. From the outset, nightly washing is essential and abrasions, blisters, bites and stings must be assessed by medics and treated immediately to prevent dangerous infection. Ticks are a non-life threatening, but uncomfortable and inconvenient predator, and these too must be located and removed to prevent infection occurring. Competitors must also eat and get ready for sleep before nightfall if at all possible. Race staff provides hot water, so re-hydrating food is relatively simple. Pitching the hammock can be a bit more challenging and time spent familiarizing oneself with this (and all kit) is time well spent. It makes a lot of sense to treat the hammock with mosquito repellent (and to ensure that the mosquito net is intact) before leaving home, as it does minimize insect bites during the night. The final task is to prepare the following day's kit.

This deceptive short first stage has a disproportionate effect on the morale of the field. As the competitors go to bed for the first night under the jungle canopy in their hammock, they contemplate another day tomorrow that is one-third longer than the enormous feat just accomplished. Earplugs are worth considering as part of the runner's kit; the jungle likes to sing at night (as do some fellow competitors, especially the Brazilians).

**BELOW** One of the many swamp crossings in the jungle.

## STAGE 2 – LIFE IN THE JUNGLE

At 24.5km, the cut-off time for Stage 2 is 11 hours 30 minutes. The terrain and conditions are similar to Stage 1, but the day is 8.5km longer and includes two swamps. Runners who struggled to complete Stage 1 have a hard road ahead.

Yet it is always surprising how versatile the human body and mind can be, and runners often find themselves striking a rhythm on Stage 2 in the Jungle Marathon. The terrain is starting to feel a bit more familiar; some of the sounds seem a bit less intimidating and some even comfortingly familiar. A day behind you in a multi-stage event is a powerful psychological booster.

As the race progresses and blisters worsen and feet become more and more bruised, competitors crave the respite of open sandals or bare feet. The jungle floor, however, is not the place to be placing tender skin. Any flesh near ground level acts as an instant magnet to the multitude of bugs that scourge that surface for food. Both sitting and walking without fully covered shoes are activities that are actively discouraged during the Jungle Marathon.

**ABOVE** Competitors carry out evening chores, including cooking meals and washing and drying clothes.

Food and water management are important aspects of any multi-stage event. Somewhat counter-intuitively, despite the persistent rain and mist, dehydration remains a very real problem for Jungle Marathon participants. There is a maximum volume of 2.5kg of water provided at each checkpoint along the route. Runners must transfer all this water into their own drinking systems. In total, competitors are each allocated 12 litres of water per day (includes the campsite ration). Salt tablets are part of the compulsory kit list and consideration should be given to using them to supplement isotonic drinks.

Ablutions carry a separate set of challenges. Before putting on shoes at any time, competitors are warned first to check for scorpions. Then the ground below the hammock needs to be carefully scoured for nocturnal visitors before setting down a foot. Small but important things to remember upon waking in the middle of the night. It is little wonder that sleep can be elusive even after an exhausting 24km running effort.

## STAGE 3 – THE 'WILD CARD'

At 31.1km, Stage 3 notionally builds on Stage 2, adding a further 6–7km with some steep slopes near the end. However, conditions in the jungle are extremely unpredictable and require a bit of ad lib, and the race director can use her discretion to alter the course.

In 2006, the field was struggling to cope with the conditions and the decision was taken to shorten the stage by 3km. When an elite field starts to lose a disproportionate number of runners to fatigue or injury, it suggests that conditions have crossed the line from extreme to prohibitively difficult and dangerous. The race director cannot improve the conditions, so the only option is to reduce the distance to counter the other countervailing elements and guarantee a safe and balanced race. Unfortunately for those who like statistics, this essential pragmatism makes personal bests and course records meaningless.

**BELOW** Stage 4 commences with a 200m-wide fiord across a tributary of the Rio Tapajós.

## STAGE 4 – A 'REST DAY'

Stage 4 is a markedly reduced distance in preparation for the long Stage 5 the following day. The Stage 4 rest day is just 18.4km, and the cut-off is back to 10 hours 30 minutes. The trade-off for this 'easier' day is a 200m-wide river crossing right at the start. During the day, runners are likely to encounter sections of very dense jungle with many plants that will either sting or cut you. At the end of Stage 4 competitors would have run approximately 100km through the jungle.

Mental and physical fatigue is starting to take its toll. So too is the excitement and exhilaration that tomorrow is the 'Big One' and the last real hurdle before a gentle final day.

The extra time in camp, at the end of Stage 4, is utilized by competitors to firm up the strategy for the daunting Stage 5 challenge that may involve a night in the jungle. One of the biggest ambitions for most runners is to avoid that at all possible cost.

**ABOVE** In the jungle, it is impossible to keep feet dry, which potentially leads to infections and other foot problems.

## STAGE 5 – THE BIG ONE

The race has been building to the epic adventure that is Stage 5: the 83km non-stop leg with its cut-off time of 36 hours. The stage is a mix of 45km of tough jungle trail and 38km of open plantation trails.

The 36-hour time limit is generous, mostly to mitigate the risk of runners getting caught out in the 'dark zone' (situated 34km from the start). The area between Checkpoint 4 and 5 is relatively heavily populated with jaguar. On occasion, they have been known to wander onto the trail. Therefore, it is simply not safe to permit runners to be at risk of being caught in this 'dark zone' during nightfall.

In order to minimize this risk, race organizers impose an additional cut-off point at 4pm; runners arriving at Checkpoint 4 from 4pm must spend the night there and proceed the next day in daylight hours. This strategy has its weaknesses. It does not, for example, prevent the runner who passed checkpoint 4 at 3.30pm from becoming injured and finding him or herself in precisely the place he or she is not supposed to be as night falls.

Those who do proceed past checkpoint 4 before 4pm (and do not sustain serious injury in jaguar territory), are permitted to continue to race through the night. The trail is reasonably well defined, following the glowing chemical sticks to light the way, but this is the jungle. There is no clear, straight route and, given the twisting and turning nature of the trail, there are frequent periods when there is not a glow stick in sight.

**OPPOSITE** Local families provide encouragement over the last few kilometres.

Navigation is tricky in those conditions, and it is not unheard of for competitors to make a wrong turn. There is nothing worse than the sickening realization that you have lost the trail. The panic subsides only to be replaced with a heart-sinking realization that the only safe course of action is to retrace the route to the last known marker. Hard-won ground is lost and valuable time and energy is wasted as a consequence.

These are the sorts of defining moments that differentiate extreme adventure racers from the rest of the population. The 2006 race director summed it up as:

*'Those who make it out of the jungle during daytime will do a lot of this stage in the dark. And there are parts where it is scary. Even though you are near communities it will feel as if you are in the middle of nowhere. I strongly recommend teaming up as there will be all kinds of crawly creatures at night. It's when the jungle comes to life. 4 eyes see more and will make it safer for you.'*

### STAGE SIX – TO THE FINISH LINE!

In real terms it is still a long day, but the 9-hour time limit for the final 24.8km is a walk in the park compared to the day (and night) before.

On the final day, competitors set out later than usual. Those who were cut-off at Checkpoint 4 the day before came in late and have had little time to recover before setting off again for this final stage.

**BELOW** Competitors share the joy of successfully completing the event.

The route follows the lovely shoreline and the race finish is soon within sight. The sweet smell of imminent success and the flow of adrenaline spurred by the nearing end drives competitors the last few kilometres. Battered and bruised from their battle with the jungle, competitors stumble in to Alter do Chão to complete this epic adventure.

At the end of most extreme running events, the sense of camaraderie at the finish line is palpable. At the end of the Jungle Marathon, it is different and far more intense. This is not a case of enduring an extremely difficult race. This is the survival of mankind in the jungle amidst some of the most dangerous predators known to man.

No surprise, then, that the Jungle Marathon is quite some bonding experience.

THE UNUSUAL CONDITIONS IN THE JUNGLE, including the presence of so many predators, make the proper choice of clothing more than just a matter of comfort.

**FOOTWEAR** Sturdy shoes are essential and a good fell running sole can be of great assistance in climbing slippery banks, gripping the tree bark of logs that have fallen across the trail or been strategically positioned across it to bridge creeks and areas of swamp. There are plenty of rivers and swamps that have no such luxuries, so footwear must be adaptable enough to deal with being soaking wet for long periods of time. Sweat, humidity, heat and mud conspire to defeat even the best shoe manufacturers' efforts; footwear glue is prone to dissolve in these wet and arduous conditions.

**BODYWEAR** To prevent chafing in this humid environment, clothing made of modern, light, technical fabrics are tempting. But these will not protect participants from the surrounding flora and fauna's army of weaponry from plants' razor sharp thorns, barbs and protrusions, scalpel-like grasses, tree bark as rough as sandpaper; and various bruising and piercing stumbling blocks that litter the forest floor. The obstacles, coupled with those of the 2.5 million insect species that bite, all provide persuasive reasons for participants in this event to cover up in long tops and trousers made of hardy and tear-proof fabric.

As the hands are particularly vulnerable to the conditions, often making contact with the ground or branches as runners are forced to reach out to break a fall or steady themselves, gloves are worth considering as well.

**HEADWEAR** A decent sunhat is essential. Parts of the race are outside the canopy of the rainforest and the sun is fiercely hot. Under cover of the rainforest, a hat can provide welcome protection from bugs and reptiles that have an unwelcome tendency to drop unexpectedly from the trees above.

'The primary contact with such a hostile environment should be through the soles of ones shoes.'
**Dari Salon, race finisher (2004)**

# ATACAMA
# CROSSING

THE ATACAMA CROSSING is a multi-stage, self-sufficiency, desert race that takes place in some of the driest conditions on earth. The Atcama Desert course changes every year, which adds to the sense of unknown in this foreign environment. However, the key elements of the event remain constant: clear skies, high altitude, extreme temperature variations and generally tough running conditions over six stages (including an 80km stage).

The Atcama Desert sits in the 'rain shadow' of the Andes. The average annual precipitation is 0.1mm, at the very limit of measurable rainfall. In some areas, there has been no recorded rainfall at all. Research indicates that the desert has been this dry for over 20 million years. It has created an environment and terrain so alien that NASA uses it for testing extra-planetary vehicles.

**ABOVE** Crossing the Chilean salt flats during the last few kilometres.

**OPPOSITE** Stunning landscape in the Valle de la Luna (Valley of the Moon) within the world's driest desert.

The 2006 course start line was near Machuca, at an altitude of 4,110m. Competitors set off in the icy cold, early morning on the 32km first stage, which was a descent to 2,700m. There were multiple bitterly cold river crossings, which added to the already extreme conditions.

The terrain over the middle stages is a mix of canyons, knee-deep water, sand dunes and monotonous stretches of salt flats. It is testing, but competitors are treated to stunning vistas of volcanoes and red peaks. They also must endure the inevitable, interminable salt flats and the ferocious winds that haunt them.

The fifth and penultimate stage is the longest day: an 80km ultra-marathon across more salt flats, sand dunes, canyons and rivers, and an area of desert known as the Valley of the Moon.

At some point, most competitors will be forced to choose whether to press on through the biting cold night without stopping, or to camp at a checkpoint with all the comforts of a fire, warm food and a sleeping bag. Any rest, of course, comes at the price of a longer stage overall.

The sixth and final stage tends to be a surprisingly short and gentle final stretch (11km in 2006) to the finish line in the town of San Pedro de Atacama.

The fastest overall completion time is around 28 hours and the slowest around 70 hours. At a total distance of 250km, the Atacama Crossing is the equivalent distance of the entire width of Chile. The vast expanse of extraterrestrial landscape provides the organizers with an infinite range of options for staging the most challenging of ultramarathon courses.

## KEY DATA

**RACE** Atacama Crossing
**LOCATION** Atacama Desert (Chile)
**DISTANCE** 250km (150 miles), 6 stages
**DATES** March/August (alternate by year)
**TOTAL ASCENT** Course varies each year
**TOTAL DESCENT** Course varies each year
**KEY CHARACTERISTICS** Multi-terrain, self-sufficiency race through the driest desert on Earth at an altitude greater than 1,610m (5,280ft)
**RACE RECORDS** Course varies each year
**FIELD (APPROX)** 150–200
**CLIMATE** Extremely dry. Day: 40°C (100°F); Night: sub-zero
**FINISHERS** 80% of starters
**RACE DIRECTOR** Mary K. Gadams
**EMAIL** info@racingtheplanet.com
**WEB** www.4deserts.com

**'It does not matter** how slow you go, as long as you don't stop.'
**Confucius**

# INCA TRAIL
# **MARATHON**

THE INCA TRAIL is the track that links the ancient mountain city of Machu Picchu, high in the Andes of Peru, to the nearest town of Llactapta and on to bustling Cusco. The Inca Trail Marathon follows the uneven, cobbled Inca path across three mountain passes exceeding 3,600m in height. Participants in the Marathon endeavour to cover the 44.2km route – a 3–4 day trek by normal standards – in just a few hours. The backdrop provided by the high granite mountains, lush flora, majestic ruins and eyrie mists makes this one of the most magnificent marathons in the world.

The Inca Trail Marathon starts beside a large rock on the outskirts of Llactapta (2,440m). From there it is a 7km, undulating climb to the last settlement on the trail, Wayllabamba. Across the river, the trail proceeds to the start of the first big climb of 1,400m over 9km. At the top, competitors reach the unnervingly named 'Dead Woman's Pass'.

Along the trail, competitors run through lush, thick forest conditions until they reach the tree line at 3,780m and the beginning of alpine conditions. The first pass at 4,200m is the highest point on the course. Oxygen is scarce at that altitude and few competitors would actually run that part.

From the highest pass, it is straight downhill for some way. The route is steep, uneven and the large carved stone steps are difficult to navigate. After a descent of more than 400m, the route leads into a second climb to the next pass at 3,990m. This overlooks the *Runkuraqay* ruins, which provide a tantalizing taster of things to come. The third and final pass is above the *Phuyupatamarca* ruins. By now, competitors are fatigued and the effects of oxygen deprivation are marked.

From the third and final pass, the route descends back down to below the tree line via '1300 Steps'. Each step brings a minute increase in temperature, humidity and wildlife until, at the end, the entire atmosphere has changed. Conditions for running improve

## KEY DATA

RACE  Inca Trail Marathon
LOCATION  Llactapta (Peru)
DISTANCE  44.2km (27.5 miles), single stage
DATE  July
TOTAL ASCENT  2,150m (7,050ft)
TOTAL DESCENT  2,100m (6,890ft)
KEY CHARACTERISTICS  High altitude, mountain run over steep trails to Machu Picchu
RACE RECORDS  Male 5:19, Female 6:37
FIELD (APPROX)  40
CLIMATE  26°C–0°C (80°–32°F)
FINISHERS  100% of starters
RACE DIRECTOR  Devy Reinstein
EMAIL  info@andesadventures.com
WEB  www.andesadventures.com

considerably as well over the last few kilometres of the event.

The high point of the Inca Trail Marathon is the final short climb to the 'Gateway of the Sun', which leads to the first viewpoint for the magnificent Machu Picchu. From there, it is but an easy 350m descent to the finish line and the famed 'lost city' ruins.

Running the Inca Trail is like taking a step back in time. One can imagine the relays of Inca *chasqui* (messengers) pounding the cobblestone paths to deliver important messages to keep the empire running. It is claimed the *chasqui* runners could relay a parcel from Cusco to Quito, a distance in excess of 1,600km as the crow flies, in under a week! Whilst the speed may be a little exaggerated, there is little doubt that the local *chasqui* were true ultra runners of their time.

**OPPOSITE AND ABOVE** The steep slopes of Huayana Picchu mountain. Passing through the entrance to Machu Picchu.

## 'Then up the ladder of the earth I climbed; through the barbed jungle's thickets; until I reached you Machu Picchu.'
**Pablo Neruda (Chilean poet, Nobel Prize for Literature 1971)**

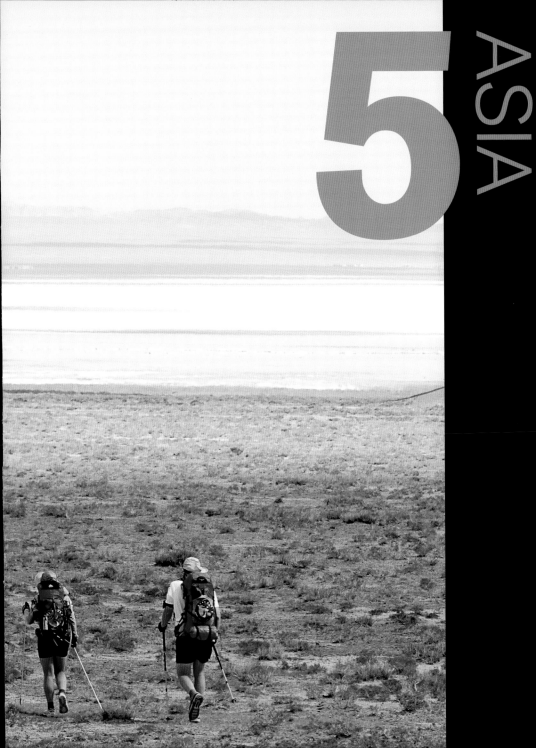

# **EVEREST**
# MARATHON

**PAGES 100/101** Traversing over grasslands towards large salt flats during the Gobi March.

**ABOVE** A yak train carries runners' kit bags up towards Mount Everest.

MT EVEREST (SAGARMATHA/CHOMOLUNGMA) is the highest mountain on earth. The Everest Marathon takes place in its shadow, high in the Himalayan range that marks the border between the mountain kingdom of Nepal and the mystical plateaus of Tibet.

Mountain climbers share the same astounding courage and passion that motivates extreme runners. Both are on a quest to achieve the unachievable and to experience the extraordinary. For the climber, ascending Mt Everest is the ultimate quest. At 8,848m, Mt Everest

# 'You don't have to be a fantastic hero to do certain things - to compete. You can be just an ordinary chap, sufficiently motivated to reach challenging goals.'

**Sir Edmund Hillary**

is the highest summit on earth, as measured above sea level. Climbers describe the conquest of Everest as having 'an everlasting, profound impact'. For the runner, the Everest Marathon experience is equally enduring and powerful, due in part to the challenging conditions and in part to the presence of Everest itself. This race is the extreme running world's own, ultimate summit.

Any traveller to the Everest region must contend with the effects of high altitude. Altitude sickness commonly occurs in individuals at altitudes of 2,400m and above. The average altitude of the Everest Marathon is approximately 4,000m and the start line is at 5,184m. The effects of the altitude are compounded by extreme physical exertion.

Running a marathon, like climbing a mountain, qualifies as extreme physical exertion for most people. Therefore, acclimatization is a critical aspect of race preparation. However, acclimatization takes time and, consequently, competitiors must contend with the effects on the body of a 16-day trek to the start line, in taxing conditions replete with bugs and bacteria. Couple with those factors the extreme cold caused by high-altitude conditions, and the factors are in place for a difficult and demanding adventure race.

The region is spectacularly beautiful. The 1,287km Himalayan range is home not only to Everest but to a total of eight of the world's ten highest peaks. The region's inhabitants are the Sherpa people, an ethic mountain group indigenous to the mountain regions of Nepal, who originally migrated from eastern Tibet more than 500 years ago. The Sherpa follow Tibetan Buddhism and the *gompas* (temples) and *chortens* (stupas) are dotted throughout the foothills, together with the fluttering prayer flags in vivid blue, red, green, yellow

## RACE DIRECTOR'S OPENING

WHEN THE EVEREST MARATHON started in 1987, there were very few adventure races in existence; it was considered to be quite a lunatic event.

The race was the brain-child of two British trekkers who organised an impromptu race along the main trekking trail to Everest in 1985. The course was from the Sherpa town, Namche Bazaar, to the Buddhist monastery at Tengboche and back.

The current start line of the Everest Marathon, at the old Everest base camp at Gorak Shep (5,184m), has placed the event in the *Guinness Book of Records* as 'the marathon with the highest start'. But it is Mt Everest itself that lures runners to visit this place, as it is one that many have dreamed of since childhood.

One of the principal reasons for organizing the Everest Marathon is to raise money for health and educational projects in rural Nepal through the race charity (the Everest Marathon Fund), which has raised almost half a million pounds for grass roots development projects in one of the poorest countries in the world.

With outstanding Himalayan scenery, fun-loving, friendly locals and the camaraderie which develops between runners, the Everest Marathon is much more than just a race. It is an occasion that has proved to be a life-changing event in many people's lives.

**Diana Penny Sherpani**
RACE DIRECTOR

and white, and small carved *mani* stones piled in prayer to the Tibetan deities. There is also the odd yak train to avoid while running the marathon.

The Sherpas are much more than interesting spectators in the Everest Marathon. They are integral to the race organization and function. Also, Nepali runners — accustomed as they are to the high altitude and local running conditions — often compete in the event and win, currently holding six of the top 10 race times in race history. It is difficult to begrudge their success: hearing the jubilant crowd at the finish line welcoming the local hero is a treat in itself.

## Kathmandu Capers

Like many extreme running events located in remote corners of the world, it takes some effort to reach the start line for the Everest marathon.

This journey commences in the Nepalese capital of Kathmandu. Kathmandu is both a modern diplomat town and an ancient place of history and tradition. Kathmandu's 'old' city is the site of multiple historic Buddhist and Hindu temples and palaces, many dating back to the 17th century.

BELOW Competitors approaching Namche Bazaar, location of the marathon finish line.

**KEY DATA**

**RACE** Everest Marathon
**LOCATION** Sagarmatha National Park (Nepal)
**DISTANCE** 42.2km, single stage
**DATE** November
**TOTAL ASCENT** 400m (1,300ft)
**TOTAL DESCENT** 3,695m (12,100ft)
**KEY CHARACTERISTICS** High altitude start at Gorak Shep 5,184m (17,000ft), near Everest Base Camp, finishing in Namche Bazaar 3,346m (11,300ft). 16-day trek to the start line!
**RACE RECORDS** Male 3:50, Female 5:16
**FIELD (APPROX)** 75 (+ 10 Nepalese runners)
**CLIMATE** -20°C (-4°F) to +20°C (68°F) less any wind chill; snow, sleet or rain possible
**FINISHERS** 90% of starters
**RACE DIRECTOR** Diana Penny Sherpani
**EMAIL** sherpa@bufoventures.co.uk
**WEB** www.everestmarathon.org.uk

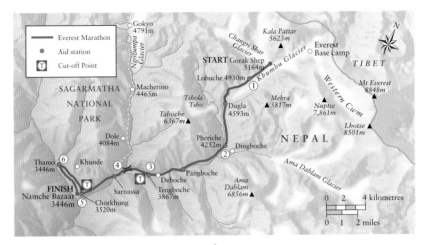

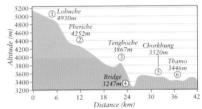

Upon arrival in the intriguing Kathmandu Valley, race participants are required to make their way to a pre-designated hotel (Hotel Shanker in 'old' Kathmandu) for introductions and an official race briefing. It is there that the reality of the coming weeks becomes apparent. Tacked to a pin board are lists that allocate participants to trekking groups, tent partners and race doctors. Due to the number of competitors (and Sherpa guides, porters, kitchen staff and support crew), separate trekking groups are required to minimize congestion on the trek in.

As a warm-up to the event, the race organizers host a 15km 'fun run' through the (polluted) streets of the city on the day before leaving Kathmandu. If nothing else, this puts participants in the mood for the fresh mountain air that awaits them outside the city limits.

# Retracing Hillary's Footprints

The journey to the race start line has three main components. As the race starts from Gorak Shep, the original base camp of Everest, the 16-day journey follows the route of the early climbing expeditions into Mt Everest Base Camp. It starts with the combined plane ride and trek to Namche Bazaar, then the week-long side trek up to the picturesque lakes and stunning vistas at Gokyo and, finally, the race course in reverse up to Gorak Shep.

The ever-present prospect of viewing the world's highest point makes the walk into Everest more of a pilgrimage than a trek.

## GATEWAY TO KHUMBU

The Everest region is called the Khumbu. Race competitors are transported from Kathmandu to Lukla 2,850m, which leads to the gateway to the Khumbu.

The small passenger plane journey is somewhat treacherous and more than a little thrilling. Built in 1964, the mountainside airstrip is famed for its 'controlled crash' landing. With no radio beacons for guidance, everything is down to pilot skill and judgement. (Naturally, this is explained to race competitors in great detail at the race briefing in Kathmandu.)

Participants trek in convoy, dispersed at sociable but uncongested intervals along the trail, from Lukla towards Mt Everest. On the second day of the trek, the party passes through Monjo, the gateway to the Sagarmatha National Park and entrance to the Khumbu (Everest region).

The English name for the region's namesake mountain was given in 1865 by the then Surveyor General, Andrew Waugh. He named the mountain after his predecessor, Sir George Everest, who oversaw the great survey of India between 1823 and 1843. In Nepali, Mt Everest is called Sagarmatha, which means 'Head Above all Others' and Tibetans and Sherpas call it Chomolungma, which means 'Mother Goddess of the World' – both of which are considerably more apt than the English name.

About 90 per cent of the Nepalese population is Hindu, as is evident in the prevalence of Hindu temples in the Kathmandu Valley. Within the Everest region, this proportion changes dramatically and the local Sherpa and Tamang follow Tibetan Buddhism. The preferred Tibetan Buddhist icons of *mani* walls and prayer flags suddenly dominate the scenery and *gompas* are commonplace.

Several hours from the gateway to the Kumbu is Namche Bazaar, a hillside town perched at 3,446m. Namche Bazaar is set in a natural amphitheatre

**BELOW** Everyone dines together during the trek in to the start line.

on the mountainside and is the last significant Sherpa village before Mt Everest. It is also the Everest Marathon race headquarters and the location of the finish line. From a vantage point just above the village, participants are treated to their first views of the magnificent Ama Dablam and Mt Everest in the distance.

The rest day at Namche Bazaar provides a useful opportunity for competitors to recce the 10km circuit, called 'Thamo Loop', which is the final section of the actual marathon.

## HOT LEMON DRINK 'RELAY'

From Namche Bazaar, the race competitors need to climb 300–500m daily, to reach the start line altitude of 5,164m at Gorek Shep. Every other day is set aside for acclimatization.

For the duration of the trek to the start line, each day commences with a warm and welcome 'bed tea'. 'Bed tea' is delivered to participants in their tents at around 6am (sunrise). Muesli or porridge is delivered an hour later.

On trekking days, the porters head off by 6.30am, taking with them competitors' kit bags, neither of which are seen again until competitors reach the next campsite in the evening. Then, the entire party of race participants tends to set off together,

**ABOVE** Runners clambering over glacier moraine – with a spectacular view towards the south-east ridge of Mt Everest.

at a more civilized hour. Before long, individual groups break away, taking comfort stops and hot lemon drink stops at the numerous teahouses along the route. The daily trek varies from four to seven hours. To the mild amusement of some, a few keen runners head off for a short evening run upon reaching camp.

The participants reach camp in plenty of time for a daily wash, medical check and any necessary gear maintenance. Nightly communal dinners take place in the mess tent. The meals, prepared by the event chef, are pleasant – if you like potato. As it is midsummer, the days are warm. But being an alpine environment, the nights can be bitterly cold. Evening conversation is often cut short because of the cold, as participants drift off to the warmth of their sleeping bags by sunset.

'The panorama stretches well into the distance, a blend of glaciers and grass, rock, snow and ice. Sunsets can be unforgettable here…'
Jamie McGuinness, *Trekking in the Everest Region* (1998)

# '...those thousands of peaks, climbed and unclimbed, of every size and order of difficulty, where we each of us may find our own Mt. Everest.'

**H W Tilman, *Mount Everest* (1938)**

During the early days of the 'trekking in' stage of the event, participants' thoughts and conversations are centred not on the marathon but on the distant views of the Himalayas and the local Nepali people with their cheerful 'Namaste' greeting. Four days on, as participants approach the village of Gokyo at 4,791m, the reality of running a marathon at this high altitude starts to strike home.

Nonetheless, there will be a good number of runners who will be sufficiently acclimatized to scale nearby Gokyo Ri at 5,483m to take in some of the best views of Mt Everest available anywhere in the Khumbu.

## OLD EVEREST BASE CAMP – THE START LINE

After a night at Gokyo, participants descend from the Gokyo valley and rejoin the actual marathon route near the famous Tengboche monastery at 3,867m. The route itself is unmarked on race day. During the final week before actual race day, participants do cover much of the marathon route. Many anxiously survey the trail in an effort to be at least a little prepared for race-day navigation challenges and to contemplate particular obstacles and more difficult sections of the course.

The eve of the race is spent in the bleak campsite at Lobuche. There, competitors undergo a series of medical tests to ensure that they are healthy and sufficiently acclimatized to start the race.

For those hardy souls, there is another side adventure in store. The old Everest Base Camp at Gorak Shep, which is simply two lodges at the edge of the Khumbu Glacier, is within two to three hours' walking distance of Lobuche. From there, participants are able to summit Kalar Pattar, at 5,623m, in another one to two hours. The summit of Kala Pattar is the closest that participants will come to the summit of Everest during the event; it is a mere 3,200m from the top. This lofty ridge provides a magnificent altar, from which the faithful can worship the mountain. The racing pulse and heavy breathing caused by the exertion of the climb up Kala Pattar gives a renewed appreciation for those who have reached its summit.

To many participants in the Everest Marathon, the aspiration to set eyes on Mt Everest is as much of a driver as the race itself. Whether you are a mountain climber or not, there is something undeniably captivating about the monument that is the highest point on earth.

THE UNSPOKEN FEAR for every runner is to develop any ailments close to the Everest Marathon start, the biggest concern being altitude. Even elite athletes are not immune.

*'It is still extremely difficult to know who is likely to be struck down by it [Acute Mountain Sickness]. It can happen equally to the young or elderly, to the fit or not so fit.'*
AJ POLLARD & DR MURDOCH, *THE HIGH ALTITUDE MEDICINE HANDBOOK* (1997)

Lobuche 4,930m, set on the side of the Khumbu Glacier, is the second to last camp and site of the final rest day. It is an inhospitable campsite and snow falls are frequent.

In 1995, it was here that the decision was taken to reduce the race to a half marathon due to freak snows and avalanche dangers.

At Lobuche, almost everyone will suffer some effects of altitude (headache, poor sleep, shortness of breath) and, nearly every year, some competitors are taken down to lower altitude during the night because of AMS (altitude mountain sickness). In 1999, one runner was evacuated inside a pressurized 'gammow bag'.

The day before the race, every runner is required to undergo a medical check at Labouche, before being permitted to trek up to the start at Gorak Shep. After a chest examination and some acclimatization 'balancing acts', successful runners are finally handed their race numbers.

# A Race Day Diary

4AM  I awoke to the sound of my wristwatch alarm. I quickly consumed my pre-race breakfast (two carbo drinks, a sports bar and two squeezies) and tried to get back to sleep. Sleep is difficult at Gorak Shep where the air pressure, and therefore the amount of oxygen, is half about what it is at sea level. My resting pulse had risen to 92 beats per minute, compared to 54 beats per minute in Kathmandu. During the trek up here, I lost three kilograms of body weight. (I will lose a further two kilograms during the race itself.) The altitude up here consumes body fat at an alarming rate.

6:00AM  A whistle blew. Rice pudding and tea were thrust into the tent. We had 45 minutes to stay warm. I had slept in my running gear with shoes inside the sleeping bag. I noticed my water bottle was frozen. Outside it had snowed and the temperature was minus 20° Celsius.

6:45AM  A second whistle. Everyone left their tents and walked to the start area 20 metres away. I was wearing as little as possible given the conditions: one layer of merino clothing, a windbreaker, a balaclava and two pairs of thermal gloves. Race numbers were called. 'Forty-one!' I yelled. There were 75 hardy souls in total.

7:00 AM We were off, crunching through the frozen snow, sliding over the Khumbu Glacier boulders and gasping. I took a chance and sprinted from the start, praying I could handle the cold and altitude. My gamble seemed to be working, as I passed the first five kilometre checkpoint in less than 30 minutes. Even at this stage the field had split apart.

The next four kilometres were a steep rocky descent. I tried to bypass a bridge by crossing the river at a lower point. I slipped on an icy rock and fell in – it was a fortunate move, as the freezing water numbed my throbbing knee.

After 14 kilometres we had dropped 1,000 metres. The sun was up and breathing became easier. I removed my gloves and balaclava.

**OPPOSITE** Crossing the footbridge below Tengboche Monastery.

Throughout the course there were checkpoints every five kilometres. Each one was manned by an encouraging doctor and marshal, offering sterilized water and fruit or muesli bars. I was forcing myself to drink 1 litre of fluids at each checkpoint.

After a sharp climb up to Tengboche Monastery, I reached the halfway point. I had been running for 2 hours 45 minutes and was in 16th place. This was encouraging news but I was feeling the effects of my fast start.

Shortly after Tengboche there is a 'crux' 350m climb, up the notorious 'Sarnassa Hill', and then an undulating 5 kilometres towards Namche Bazaar. Unfortunately, there is then a final 10 kilometre loop to Thamo village and back (which seemed to be inclining uphill in both directions). Spurred on by the knowledge of my race position, rather than my race fitness, I found the impetus to push forward towards the finish.

Finally, I rounded the last bend and saw the rooftops of Namche Bazaar 70m below. I reached the finish line, elated. I had survived.

**BELOW** A runner passes some holy stone cairns, memorials to Sherpas who have died whilst climbing in the region.

## The Finish

Despite the challenges of the altitude, climate and taxing trek to the start line, the majority of competitors successfully complete the Everest Marathon. Moreover, the majority of competitors finish with enormous enthusiasm, spurred on by the locals and their fellow participants.

The physical location of the finish line is the inauspicious site of a potato field, situated just inside Namche Bazaar township. Given the prevalence of potatoes in participants' diet in the preceding fortnight, it is a fitting way to finish.

As each competitor crosses the finish line, he or she is garlanded with a traditional Tibetan white silk greeting scarf, a *katar*, and the prestigious and rare Everest Marathon race medal. Participants wear both as a proud symbol that they have completed an epic journey of endurance. A journey that is much longer than the race itself, and one in which each and every participant would have encountered his or her own personal struggle and established his or her very own, unique race story.

The godfather of Mt Everest summed it up in two very different, but both equally apt, quotes. Sir Edmund Hillary said that '*It is not the mountain we conquer, but ourselves*.' He was more direct, if not less profound, upon returning to base camp immediately after his Everest summit, when he reported to his team: '*Well, we knocked the bastard off!*'

**LEFT** Passing Tibetan prayer wheels, less than a kilometre before the finish.

**BELOW** The 'potato field' finish line in the centre of Namche Bazaar.

# GOBI **MARCH**

THE GOBI DESERT straddles the border between China and Mongolia. It is one of the most hostile environments on the planet. For most of the year, it is a frozen waste-land. In the brief months of summer, it transforms into a simmering cauldron. The plains are so prone to ravaging winds that ancient traders plying the Silk Route feared to cross them. Yet the same plains are the site of the Gobi March: an annual and epic 250km multi-stage, self-sufficiency foot race.

The actual course changes every year and race organizers have unlimited options for setting each new challenge. The Gobi Desert is 1.3 million square kilo-metres of uncompromising terrain. Although famed for its open, flat, black-gravel surface, the Gobi also boasts run-off fed oases, steep-sided canyons, mountains and a small section of sand dunes to the southwest.

The terrain is extremely challenging. The weather is completely chaotic and experiencing four seasons in as many days is not at all uncommon. This is an extremely long race: competitors need carefully to manage pace and water consumption throughout. Water rations are provided only at nightly campsites and at the race checkpoints. At the campsites, however, there is also fire to heat water and food and tents to keep out the worst of the elements. All other equipment must be carried by the competitor.

The race course follows the same general format every year. Four initial stages are split evenly to cover a culmulative distance of some 170km. The first four days are the simply a prelude to the 'long one' – 80km across the desert in one or perhaps two self-imposed stages.

Most athletes use approximately 6,000 Kcal per day but carry only 2,000 Kcal per day for the event. The deficit is made up from existing body fat and muscle. Four solid days of racing rapidly expends pre-loaded carbohydrates and the body is already in a fatigued state well before the start of the 'longest day'.

## KEY DATA

**RACE** Gobi March
**LOCATION** Gobi Desert (Xinjiang province, China)
**DISTANCE** 250 kilometres (150 miles), 6 stages
**DATE** June (may vary)
**TOTAL ASCENT** Course varies each year.
**TOTAL DESCENT** Course varies each year.
**KEY CHARACTERISTICS** Mixed-terrain, multi-stage self-sufficiency race through Gobi Desert.
**RACE RECORDS** Course varies each year.
**FIELD (APPROX)** 200
**CLIMATE** Day: 40°C (100°F); Night: sub-zero.
**FINISHERS** 80% of starters.
**RACE DIRECTOR** Mary K. Gadams
**EMAIL** info@racingtheplanet.com
**WEB** www.4deserts.com

Some competitors attempt the 80km fifth stage in a single leg, which requires them to be out in the desert sun during the hottest part of the day (between 2pm and 7pm). The sun is a real danger and there is little or no shade cover on the course. Most of the field will, however, complete the 'longest day' by lunchtime the following day, having elected to sleep en route.

The Gobi Desert is known as the 'gravel desert', as it is in the main flat, rocky and covered in small, black pebbles. The conditions underfoot are uneven. This, combined with heat, moisture (sweat or river water) and sand or grit, provides a perfect recipe for blisters.

A last 'sprint' stage is to make up the final distance to 250km total. Even those who withdrew earlier in the event often will rejoin the field at the start of the final stage, if injuries permit. Those competitors will record a 'DNF', but at least they will experience the start, and the finish, of this incredibly difficult event.

**BELOW** Competitors descend the Gobi sand dunes during high winds.

# LAKE BAIKAL INTERNATIONAL
# ICE MARATHON

THE LAKE BAIKAL International Ice Marathon offers competitors the unique opportunity to race across the frozen ice surface of the largest and deepest fresh water lake in the world. The event takes place in an extraordinarily isolated part of Russia. It is based in the small town of Listvyanka, 65km south of Irkutsk (a stopover on the Trans-Siberian route).

The Marathon is just a small part of a larger winter games festival, the 'Winteriada', which includes a swimming race in the frozen lake.

Lake Baikal is vast — at 636km by 70km — and extraordinarily deep at 1,637m. It is the repository of a fifth of the world's unfrozen fresh water. It is estimated that the lake holds sufficient water to supply drinking water for every human for a period of 50 years.

The surface of the frozen lake is covered in fields of 'hummocks', small hills of ice rubble. Beneath the ice surface, geothermic springs and seismic activity cause localized melting that weakens the ice to form holes. The race 'Ice Captain' and his team of volunteers have the task of plotting a safe course. They do so the day immediately preceding the race, otherwise movements in the ice would render their effort redundant.

On race day itself, competitors are ferried by van from Listvyanka to Tankhoy train station, located on the opposite shore of Lake Baikal. Prior to the start of the race, competitors are required to partake in the precautionary ritual of 'vodka sprinkling', in order to pacify the spirits of the Lake (introducing the novel element of starting a marathon with a shot of vodka).

The course is predominantly flat, but the surface is

## KEY DATA

**RACE** Lake Baikal International Ice Marathon
**LOCATION** Lake Baikal (Listvyanka, Russia)
**DISTANCE** 42.2km (26 miles), single stage
**DATE** March
**TOTAL ASCENT** Negligible
**TOTAL DESCENT** Negligible
**KEY CHARACTERISTICS** Marathon on frozen surface of world's largest and deepest fresh-water lake
**RACE RECORDS** Male 3:08, Female: 3:54
**FIELD (APPROX)** 30
**CLIMATE** -5°C to 2°C (23°F to 35°F)
**FINISHERS** 75–80% of starters
**RACE DIRECTOR** Andreas Kiefer
**EMAIL** info@baikal-express.de
**WEB** www.baikal-marathon.de

**ABOVE** Running across the width of the world's largest and deepest fresh-water lake.

hard and uneven. Although it is mostly covered in a soft layer of snow, there are areas of highly polished ice that create conditions similar to an ice-rink. Strong winds add to the already bitingly cold temperature and provide serious resistance to progress across the Lake.

The utterly featureless landscape gives little or no sense of perspective to competitors. The finish line at the port of Listvyanka can be seen almost from the start line. It is a long, cold, lonely 42.2km trail across the barren white landscape, where progress is marked only by checkpoints positioned at 5km intervals (with hot drinks, food and, for the brave, more vodka).

The far reaches of Siberia may not be a first choice destination for many endurance athletes, who may prefer instead the warmer, and more glamorous, climes. But for those that brave the Russian winter, the reward is a fantastic race, in an area of outstanding natural beauty, on a one-off running surface.

# 'There are only a few places in the world where you can run a marathon on ice. On Lake Baikal it was harder than on Yukon in Canada.'
**Udo Möller (6th place finisher, 2005)**

# KEPLER
# **CHALLENGE**

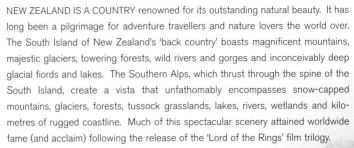

**PAGES 118/119** Running along a ridge in Fiordland National Park, with the majestic Lake Te Anau below (Kepler Challenge).

**BELOW** The race engenders a strong sense of community spirit.

NEW ZEALAND IS A COUNTRY renowned for its outstanding natural beauty. It has long been a pilgrimage for adventure travellers and nature lovers the world over. The South Island of New Zealand's 'back country' boasts magnificent mountains, majestic glaciers, towering forests, wild rivers and gorges and inconceivably deep glacial fiords and lakes. The Southern Alps, which thrust through the spine of the South Island, create a vista that unfathomably encompasses snow-capped mountains, glaciers, forests, tussock grasslands, lakes, rivers, wetlands and kilometres of rugged coastline. Much of this spectacular scenery attained worldwide fame (and acclaim) following the release of the 'Lord of the Rings' film trilogy.

The New Zealand Department of Conservation responded to the demand of locals and visitors alike, by designating nine of the country's premier walking tracks the 'Great Walks'. The 'Great Walks' take trekkers through areas of some of the best scenery in the country, if not the world. And four of the nine 'Great Walks' — including the Kepler Track — are located in the Fiordland National Park. The Fiordland National Park is now the cornerstone of the Southwest New Zealand World Heritage Area, known as Te Wahipounamu (meaning 'the place of greenstone' in Maroi). Several large and spectacularly beautiful glacier lakes dominate the park, including Lake Te Anau ('cave of the swirling water') and Lake Manapouri ('lake of the sorrowing heart').

'A cherished corner of the world where mountains and valleys compete with each other for room, where scale is almost beyond comprehension, rainfall is measured in metres and scenery encompasses the broadest width of emotions.'
**Christl McMillan et al,** *Mountains of Water - The Story of Fiordland National Park* **(1986)**

Lake Te Anau is one of the lakes that, according to Maori tradition, was dug by the Maori chieftain Rakaihautu, when he first brought his people to Southland. Legend has it he used his famous *kō* (a tool similar to a spade) to dig out Te Anau and the other principal lakes of Te Waipounamu.

The Kepler Challenge is run along the route of the Kepler Track, which starts from the glistening, pebbly shores of Lake Te Anau. From there, it is a

60km course (in walking time equating to a 3–4 day trek), which traverses terrain ranging from the lakeshore, up a steep and lengthy incline to Luxmore Hut (at 1,085m), along the exposed alpine ridge tops before the descent to the Iris Burn Hut, then along the Iris Burn glacial valley to the next hut (Moturau Hut) right on the shore of magnificent Lake Manapouri and, finally, on to the start/finish point at Dock Bay.

There is something about this race that encapsulates the essence of New Zealand and its people. Not only is it staged in one of the most spectacularly beautiful and unaffected areas of natural beauty in the world, but the event is supported by the entire local community and the sense of community spirit is inescapable. Perhaps this is because the Kepler Challenge is a local event, originally designed by the local community to commemorate their local hero. This has instilled in the local community a real sense of ownership and pride – this is their race.

**BELOW** Looking towards Jackson Peaks and Mt Luxmore from Te Anau township.

AS THEY RUN OVER tussock-covered mountain ridges, the competitors in the 60km Kepler Challenge Mountain Run are treated to views of one of the most spectacular landscapes in Australasia: the glacier-carved stony maze of lofty peaks, bush-clad valleys and jewel-like lakes of Fiordland, part of the Te Wahipounamu World Heritage Area in the South Island of New Zealand.

The race was first conceived by the small, tightly-knit Fiordland community in 1988 to commemorate the centenary of the discovery of the route between Lake Te Anau and Milford Sound by explorer Quintin MacKinnon. A similar route had been used by early Maori for their greenstone gathering expeditions. MacKinnon's discovery was the start of walking tourism in Fiordland, and the Milford Track was soon proclaimed to be the 'finest walk in the world'.

To organize a race over the Milford Track would prove too much of a logistic nightmare, however. Instead, the organizers chose the similarly spectacular Kepler Track, a Great Walk starting and finishing on the shores of Lake Te Anau. The word 'Challenge' in the name was chosen to express the fact that this race was to be foremost a personal challenge for runners. The race is run over an excellent surface but it requires months of hard training, determination, and a solid mental attitude: gut-busting ascents, hair-raising descents, the unpredictable and unforgiving Fiordland weather all add to the challenge. Top athletes complete it in under 5 hours, others take up to 12 hours; all receive an enthusiastic ovation at the finish line.

The Kepler Challenge has become the premier mountain running event in New Zealand.

The Fiordland community lives and breathes the race: the event is still organized by the volunteer non-profit community trust, and almost 200 local volunteers are involved on race day. To minimize the environmental impact the race is run to strict requirements by the Department of Conservation. The runners have the satisfaction of knowing they are also contributing to the protection of native wildlife: part of their entry fee is used by the organisers to maintain trap lines for introduced stoats and rats. As a result the threatened native birds, including bush robins, parakeets, fantails, blue duck and kiwi, may be seen more often in this part of Fiordland.

**Steve Norris**
CHAIRPERSON, KEPLER CHALLENGE ORGANISING COMMITTEE

Runners from throughout New Zealand, or further afar, now converge on this little community every December to compete in the Kepler Challenge. And each and every one of them is made to feel part of this very special community and part of something that is quintessentially New Zealand.

## History of the Event

In 1988, the local Te Anau community wanted to celebrate the centenary of the re-discovery of Milford Track by Quinton MacKinnon (a similar route had been used by the Maori people some time prior).

Following his re-discovery of the route in 1888, MacKinnon began to take guided walks over the Milford Track. His venture constituted one of the earliest examples of adventure tourism. It also opened up the region to visitors and first introduced the concept of tourism to the area. It has been said that, 'until the rediscovery of MacKinnon Pass Te Anau slumbered on the edge of the unknown'. His namesake, the McKinnon Pass, is the pass that permits walkers to cross the high-point on the Milford Track.

At a public meeting in the late 1980s, members of the local community decided to erect a statue in Te Anau in MacKinnon's honour and the necessary fundraising effort was launched.

As part of that effort, the local Fiordland Athletic Club tried to organize a run on one of the local tracks, ultimately settling on the Kepler Track. Given that MacKinnon's discovery made it possible for people to walk relatively easily and safely through the lofty Fiordland mountains to Milford Sound via the famous Milford Track, it made sense for the main fundraising event to have some association with the local trails and the spirit of discovery and adventure.

The Kepler Challenge was intended as a one-off event. It took place in December 1988, with a field of 149 runners. At the time, the current Kepler Track was still under construction and sections of the course were run through virgin tussock. However, the response to the event was so overwhelming that the committee decided to host the run annually.

The Kepler Challenge is now in its 20th year and firmly established in the international adventure racing calendar.

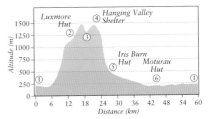

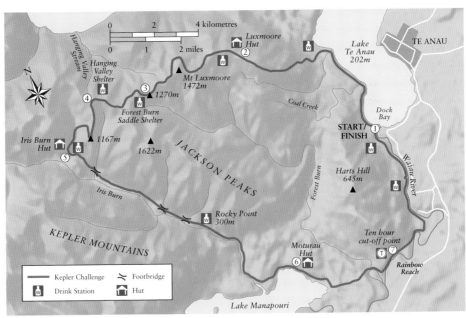

**ABOVE** Descending through typical New Zealand native bush – including beech trees and ferns.

The field is capped at 400 for the main event Kepler Challenge and 150 for the sister race, the 27km Luxmore Grunt. The race is extremely popular and in 2006 online registration closed within 30 minutes after the race reached capacity.

The local adventure and eco-tourism that MacKinnon originated, and which the Kepler Challenge has proliferated, is now a multi-million dollar industry in the region. Tourism New Zealand reports that Te Anau recorded approximately 200,000 guest nights in 2000, and one-third to two-thirds of those were overseas visitors. Not bad for a town with a population of less than 2,000 people. Needless to say, tourism is absolutely central to the local economy, and that is reason enough to commemorate Mr MacKinnon.

# Discovering the 'Back Country'

The Kepler Track, location of the Kepler Challenge, is in what is described in New Zealand parlance as the 'back country'. In general terms, 'back country' is considered to be a geographical region that is isolated, remote, undeveloped and difficult to access.

In reality, for most foreign visitors, isolated, remote, undeveloped and difficult to access are all terms that could be applied to New Zealand as a whole, not just the Southland 'back country'. They apply in particular to the small, rural township of Te Anau.

The Kepler Challenge pre-race briefing still takes place in the same town hall in which the community decided to erect the statute of MacKinnon. The race organizers share with all competitors what the event is about. They discuss the practicalities in detail (there are safety aspects that need to be managed very carefully). But in characteristic 'can do' Kiwi fashion, they chat casually through the logistics of getting the 400 strong field over 60km of difficult terrain to the finish line and back to Te Anau in time for dinner.

It is only when one leaves the township to enter the national park that the true concept of 'back country' is understood. Fiordland National Park is classic 'back country': it is vast, being one of New Zealand's largest national park, at 1,257,000 hectares, and it is wholly uninhabited by humans. It includes some of the country's most diverse and magnificent areas of native forest and indigenous grasslands. It is also home to some of New Zealand's rarest and most endangered native birds, including the Takahe and the world's only flightless parrot, the Kakapo.

Trekking in the New Zealand 'back country' can be extremely dangerous. Trekkers must be properly prepared and equipped, as there are no roads or forms of transportation in the national parks, no shops or guesthouses, and the weather can change without warning. Usually, the only accommodation is in

**BELOW** Wooden staircase at the start of the thrilling descent from Hanging Valley Shelter.

the local huts or tents. The national park huts are widely varied in style and comfort. On the Kepler Track, they are relatively new and modern with basic facilities. True 'back country' huts are actually off the Great Walks and well of the beaten track. These are a whole different experience again.

Competitors in the Kepler Challenge, however, have no need for hut accommodation. They complete the Kepler Track, from start to finish, in just one day. They pass through the three overnight huts en route, stopping to collect drinks, snacks and for toilet stops. But they are not there for sightseeing: they are there to finish a race.

## KEY DATA

**RACE:** Kepler Challenge
**LOCATION:** Te Anau (South Island, New Zealand)
**DISTANCE:** 60km (37 miles), single stage
**DATE:** December
**TOTAL ASCENT:** 1,350m (4,430ft)
**TOTAL DESCENT:** 1,350m (4,430ft)
**KEY CHARACTERISTICS:** Trail race around the spectacular Kepler Track, including two steep ascents and one punishing descent
**RACE RECORDS:** Male 4:37, Female 5:23
**FIELD (APPROX):** Limited to 400
**CLIMATE:** Possible alpine conditions – cold on passes especially if it rains or snows
**FINISHERS:** 95% of starters
**RACE DIRECTOR:** Steve Norris (Chairperson)
**CONTACT DETAILS:** email: keplerchallenge@maxnet.co.nz
**WEB:** www.keplerchallenge.co.nz

## The Race

This is a 60 kilometre race over steep mountain inclines, alpine ridges and deep, damp forest. The route is a loop course around the Jackson Peaks starting and finishing at the Lake Te Anau outlet control gates (200m). Approximately 16km of the course is uphill with a total cumulative ascent of 1,350m. The highest point on the track is the Luxmore Saddle (1,400 metres) near Kilometre 17.

The event requires careful planning and, in particular, careful consideration of weather conditions. A hot sunny day on the shores of Lake Te Anau can turn to snow up on the ridge. Competitors must prepare for all weather contingencies.

The race kicks off at 6am and runners make their way along the lakeshore through a dense beech forest, scattered with native rimu and miro. It is a gentle and undulating run along a pleasant dirt path for 5.6km to Brod Bay.

Immediately after Brod Bay, the terrain takes on a sudden and extreme change in personality. Just inland from Brod Bay begins the track to the edge of the forest and the start of the 8.2km climb to the Luxmore Hut at 1,085m. It is a long, steep and steady climb to stunning – and lethally slippery when wet – limestone bluffs. The track continues to climb above the forest to the alpine tussock on the ridge. From there, competitors can take in the panoramic view of the Te Anau basin

# 'Fiordland…one of the world's natural wonders.'

UNESCO World Heritage Committee papers

to the east, the Takitimu Mountains, and the Snowdon and Earl Mountains. That is the toughest part of the climb and from there it is a more gentle slope along the ridge to Mt Luxmore Hut. (Here, participants in the shorter Luxmore Grunt turn around and head back down the way they came back to the control gates.)

From Luxmore Hut, Kepler Challenge competitors continue their gradual climb along the ridge to Luxmore Saddle just below the summit of Mt Luxmore at 1,471m. From there to Hanging Valley Shelter, the track is very exposed and passes through nine avalanche paths. The locals will tell you that *'the wind can blow you off your feet'* in this section. At the shelter the descent begins. A series of knee-crippling zigzags heads down into the Iris Burn valley.

Back in the valley, the tussock-topped alpine ridge becomes a distant memory as the forest crowds back in around the track. Competitors pass by the Iris Burn

**OPPOSITE** Traversing snowdrifts around the side of Mt Luxmore.

**BELOW** Competitors just after Luxmore Hut.

Hut, at a much lower and more temperate 497m, sited in a large clearing with brilliant views up the valley. The total distance from Luxmore Hut to Iris Burn is 14.6km. It is a thrilling section to run.

The next part of the course is even longer, with a 16.2km course from Iris Burn Hut to the next accommodation stop (for trekkers at least). From Iris Burn Hut, it is a direct descent back into the beech forest, riverside clearings and the gorge. The track eventually descends to Lake Manapouri, then turns into lowland beech and podocarp forest. Next, competitors follow the magnificent lakeshore to Shallow Bay and, eventually, Moturau Hut located on the beach. This is the final hut on the walk and competitors will be spurred on by the knowledge that it is not more than a 'one-day walk' to the end of the track.

The next 6km to Rainbow Reach (the 10-hour cut-off point) is a gentle 'stroll' through the beech forest, where the track passes through swampy wetlands as well as beech forest. At Rainbow Reach is a swing bridge that signals the end is close by. It is a mere 10km from the swing bridge along the track back to the Control Gates and the finish line. The terrain is flat, the weather usually mild, and there are terrific forest and river views (and trout fishing) along the way.

Carsten Joergensen, the 2006 race winner, sums up the latter running stages: *'What they say about the last, relatively flat section of the race being the hardest is true: it was beautiful for three hours and awful for the last hour-and-a-half when I ran only on will power'.* The 2006 runner-up, Martin Lukes, provides an equally apt account of the race when he stated: *'It was bloody hard work'.*

## A Uniquely New Zealand Experience

Fiordland National Park is a truly spectacular corner of New Zealand, encompassing all the vivid and spectacular sights, including magnificent mountains, lakes, fiords and rainforests, within its protected boundaries. The park, and its bird life and other flora and fauna, is carefully managed and protected by the Department of Conservation. For what New Zealand may lack in ancient and historic architecture and civilization, it makes up for in natural history and natural beauty.

Like the land, the people of New Zealand are refreshingly unaffected and straightforward. Members of the local community, both young and old, come out to participate in the Kepler Challenge event, because in New Zealand that is just what you do.

**BELOW** Kepler Challenge finishers' medals – a highly coveted possession.

# TE HOUTAEWA
# **CHALLENGE**

THE TE HOUTAEWA CHALLENGE takes place on 90 Mile Beach, which is located on the western coast of the North Auckland Peninsula. The unspoiled sandy beach curves its way up the western shoreline almost to Cape Reinga, the northern-most tip of New Zealand.

The event was established 15 years ago and is based on the ancient myth of a great Maori extreme runner Te Houtaewa. The Maori proverb: *E kore e mau i koe, He wae kai pakiaka* ('a foot accustomed to running over roots makes the speediest runner') sums up both the admiration and reproach that surrounds Te Houtaewa's feat.

Legend has it that Te Houtaewa's mother, when preparing a *hangi* (earth oven), asked her son to collect some *kumara* (sweet potato) for dinner. Instead of digging up *kumara* from the nearby crop at Te Kao, Te Houtaewa ran to Ahipara at the southern end of Te Oneroa a Tohe (90 Mile Beach) and stole some from the storehouses of the local Te Rarawa people. He raced back up the beach with his

**BELOW** The famed 90 Mile Beach ultramarathon takes place on a long, single stretch of hard, flat sand.

booty, evading capture. He set off a conflict between the people of Ahipara and the tribe of Te Houtaewa.

In more peaceful modern times, runners in the Te Houtaewa Challenge are transported by bus from the nearest township of Kaitaia to the start of the event at the northern end of the magnificent 90 Mile Beach. At the start line, the local Maori tribe (to which Te Houtaewa belonged) performs a stirring haka-like challenge to the field of competitors. In a ceremonial tribute to the legend of Te Houtaewa, one of the competitors is given a *kumara* to carry to the finish line at Ahipara, the southern-most end of the beach. The purpose of the gesture is to '*return the kumara to Ahipara in a reverse of Te Houtaewa's act – an act of reparation, of reconciliation, of restitution.*'

The race starts at 7am, a few hours after the tide has turned to go out. The start line is marked with a literal line in the sand. The 60km course is entirely run on hard flat sand. The ultra-marathon course route heads south down the beautiful arching beach of white sand from Maunganui Bluff to Paripari Domain in Ahipara. The timing of the event is designed to optimize conditions, combining both firm sand and a track close to the water (to permit competitors to benefit from the sea breezes). Support stations are set up every 3km providing water, bananas and first aid.

The Te Houtaewa Challenge offers extreme runners a unique ultra-marathon course and setting in a unique corner of the world, where this beautiful 90 Mile Beach is also a designated road upon which normal road rules apply.

## KEY DATA

RACE  Te Houtaewa Challenge
LOCATION  90 Mile Beach (Kaitaia, New Zealand)
DISTANCE  60km (38 miles), single stage
DATE  March
TOTAL ASCENT  Negligible
TOTAL DESCENT  Negligible
KEY CHARACTERISTICS  Ultramarathon along one length of beach on hard flat white sand
RACE RECORDS  Male: 3:55, Female 4:34
FIELD (APPROX)  30
CLIMATE  20°C (68°F)
FINISHERS  95% of starters.
RACE DIRECTOR  Peter Kitchen
EMAIL  TeHoutaewa@xtra.co.nz
WEB  www.newzealand-marathon.co.nz

**ABOVE** The race is timed to optimise the opportunity to run on firm sand close to the sea's edge.

'It's elevating and humbling at the same time. Running along a beach at sunrise with no other footprints in the sand, you realize the vastness of creation, your own insignificant space in the plan.'
**Sister Marion Irvine (US Olympic Marathon trials qualifier)**

# BOGONG TO HOTHAM
# **TRAIL RUN**

THE BOGONG HIGH PLAINS are an adventure playground in an area of outstanding natural beauty, known as the 'Roof Top' of Australia. In winter, the area is a thriving ski resort. In summer, it boasts some of the most spectacular tramping trails in the country, one of which has become host to the 64km Bogong to Hotham 'Roof Top Run'.

The Alpine Walking Trail begins from the base of Mt Bogong and continues to the top of Mt Hotham. It is the legendry setting for a foot race across what is described as 'the most gruelling course in Australia'. Trekkers take up to a week to traverse the 64km route: determined adventure runners try to do so within the hours of daylight in one day. That said, 40–50 per cent will fail.

The event commemorates the courageous, single-day crossing attempt that was made by cross-country skier, Charles Derrick.

Derrick set out from Mountain Creek (at the foot of Mt Bogong) to Mt Hotham in winter and on skis. His endurance and resolve proved to be no match for the horrendous conditions and he perished within a few kilometres of his goal. In 1984, Russell Bulman – founder of the Australian 'Rooftop Runners' group – created the first foot race following Derrick's route.

The course begins at Mountain Creek car park (585m). The first few kilometres are easy running on good tracks up to the first major ascent: the aptly named 'Staircase Spur'. From there it is a steep and steady 1,300m rise over 6km to the top of Mt Bogong (1,986m), Victoria's highest peak. From the summit, it is a rapid 'quad-busting' descent back down towards Big River.

Competitors must ford the river before the daunting climb up Duanne Spur to the top of Mt Nelse. From there, it is a pleasant track running once again through to Langford Gap. Langford Gap is the halfway mark in the event and a significant time checkpoint. Competitors who successfully make the cut-off (and nearly half the field do not) carry on across the Bogong High Plains, descend into the Cobungra Gap, before the final ascent to the finish at Mt Hotham summit (1,860m).

The Bogong to Hotham Ultra is not a race that generates much fanfare. The field is relatively small and many are repeat entrants. This gives the race a family-like atmosphere. In addition, the demanding cut-off time at the Langford Gap proves to be a strong, unifying force. Many in the field must face a difficult decision whether or not to continue beyond that point. But the small number that does continue and successfully reaches Mt Hotham will join a very small and elite group of extraordinary sportsmen and women. Their reward is the personal knowledge that in a tough country, they have conquered one of the toughest trails of all.

## KEY DATA

**RACE** Bogong to Hotham Trail Run
**LOCATION** Mount Bogong (Victoria, Australia)
**DISTANCE** 64km (40 miles), single stage
**DATE** January
**TOTAL ASCENT** 3,000m (9,840ft)
**TOTAL DESCENT** 2,000m (6,560ft)
**KEY CHARACTERISTICS** Mountainous trail race over footpaths and 4WD tracks
**RACE RECORDS** Male 6:41, Female 8:29
**FIELD (APPROX)** Limited to 60
**CLIMATE** 20°C (68°F)
**FINISHERS** 60% of starters
**RACE DIRECTOR** Michael Grayling
**EMAIL** jlindsa1@bigpond.net.au
**WEB** www.bogong.ultraoz.com

# 'It's the best race in Australia.'
**Jonathan Worsick (Two-time race winner)**

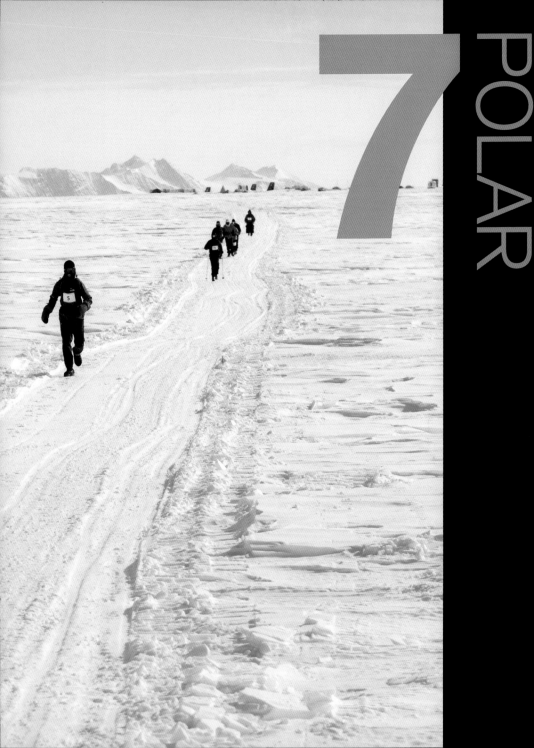

# ANTARCTICA
# **MARATHON**

THE ANTARCTIC CONTINENT represents our planet in its purest form.

The Continent keeps its silent vigil as one of the least explored and least visted corners of earth. It is situated at the furthest point of the Southern Hemisphere and is guarded on all flanks by the trecherous southern oceans. Antarctica has no airport or sea port. It simply has the natural ice shelf and bays that have existed for millions of years.

The Antarctica Marathon provides an opportunity for runners to compete in what is, on average, the coldest, driest, and windiest continent. And it has the highest average elevation. Its unique conditions have created an exceptionally inhospitable environment for such an event. There is very little precipitation (beyond the coastline), and the continent is technically the largest desert in the world. In summer, 98% of Antarctica remains covered in ice. The ice sheet is, on average, 2.5km thick. Several kilometres of the Antarctic Marathon are run over such icy foundations as runners climb the Collins Glacier.

The sea that currently surrounds Antarctica is vast, deep and cold. If the Antarctic ice were to melt, this sea (and the world's sea levels) would rise about 60m. As a reminder of this, thousands of brilliant blue-white ice massives rise from the sea to stand guard over every entry port to the Continent. These freshwater towers of ice are magnificent. They crowd the bays in every shape and size imaginable. In all the years that humankind has built great monuments to its gods, it has never recreated the spectacle that Mother Nature patiently moulds in the Antarctic. It is this indomitable sea and its protective bergs that stand between competitiors and the start line for the Antarctic Marathon.

**ABOVE** A King George Island spectator voices his opinion.

One of the most intriguing and daunting features of Antarctica is that it is a vast continent that has neither state, sovereignty, citizens nor government. The environment is fully protected by international treaty, which designates the Continent *'a natural reserve, devoted to peace and science'*. As a consequence of this unusual political status, as well as the Continent's unique geographic and climatic conditions, Antarctica remains virtually uninhabited by mankind. The odd abandoned whaling station or scientific outpost (with its seasonal and temporary staff) barely register given the sheer scale of the surrounding environment. And this lack of human settlement creates an other-wordly atmosphere. It is at once calming and, because it is so alien, slightly unsettling. The sense of unease that this creates is difficult to shake, especially during the

## RACE DIRECTOR OPENING

IT STARTED AS AN INNOCENT COMMENT that was picked up in a cover story for the *Travel Agent Magazine*, the North American industry's largest trade publication, in August 1993. I said that *'we have had a group travel to every continent except Antarctica'.* Within two days of publication, I received a call from the owner of Marine Expeditions offering to co-operate in the organisation of a marathon in Antarctica. After careful research into the environmental impact of such an event, I finally travelled to Antarctica in January 1994 to identify a location and map out a course.

After consideration of three potential venues, and a series of lengthy and involved negotiations, I reached the conclusion that the Fildes Peninsula corner of King George Island offered an ideal location for the event. In terms of the terrain, the combination course of rudimentary roads and the steep and daunting route up the Collins Glacier, seemed both challenging and interesting, but also achievable through some effort and determination.

I also needed to be confident that I could successfully pull off the event, which included the arduous sea journey from Argentina and the financial risk in chartering the ships in advance.

We successfully staged the inaugural event in 1995. I said I would never do it again, but in February 2007 we ran the event for the eighth time. I admit to saying 'never again' quite often as each time it is an enormous logistical effort.

But Antarctica is a seductive partner and it has the ability to keep drawing you back to it time and again. It challenges you mentally and physically and it is those sorts of challenges that give meaning to life.

**Thom Gilligan** RACE DIRECTOR

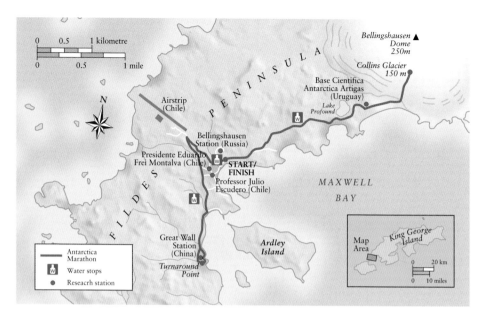

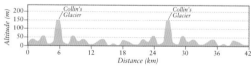

long hours alone on the race course.

The many extraordinary features that make Antarctica such a unique and special place to visit seem to be epitomized by the Antarctica Marathon. From the outset, the Continent's inaccessibility necessitates an extraordinary sea journey from Ushuaia in Tierra del Fuego, across the tumultuous Drake Passage and down to the icy climes of the South Pole. Arriving in Antarctica does not hail the end of the journey, either in the real sense or in a spiritual sense. The entire time on the Continent is packed with extraordinary side visits and wonderful opportunities to explore and discover the Antarctic allure. The race itself is another unique and special journey through the very political, geological, climatic and geographical elements that define Antarctica.

Just to be in such an environment is a life-changing adventure. To be there to run the Antarctic Marathon is magic.

## Journey to the Ice

A great explorer once said that it is not the summit that is important but the journey. Those words have never been more true than when said about the trip from Ushuaia near the southern tip of Chile to Antarctica.

# 'Antarctica is the coldest, driest, and windiest continent and has the highest average elevation… the world's last great wilderness.'

**Antarctica New Zealand (information sheet)**

Even before reaching the departure point of Ushuaia, the world's southernmost city, race participants congregate in beautiful Buenos Aires. Race organizers offer a variety of day excursions and an introductory banquet. These events provide an invaluable opportunity to meet the people who not only share your passion for adventure running, but who are about to share your (modest) floating home for the next two weeks.

After a few short days in balmy Buenos Aires, competitors are flown down to Ushuaia, where they are given half a day to explore the intriguing town and its eclectic range of shops and restaurants. The evening is spent on board a hulking Russian icebreaker, either the *Akademik Ioffe* or *Akademik Vavilov*, late in the afternoon. There is a welcome briefing and shipboard safety drill (which includes a stern warning never, ever to whistle on the bridge) and the first of many ship meals.

The boats each sleep 110 passengers. The accommodation is comfortable but by no means luxurious. The approach on board is to permit open access to the bridge and most parts of the boat. The trip is punctuated with video presentations and lectures designed to introduce visitors to the wildlife, climate and history of Antarctica. It makes for an extremely educational journey.

For five long days, the icebreakers make their slow and steady passage down to Antarctica and through the Antarctica Peninsula. Depending upon the sea conditions (and those of your own sea legs), this can be a calmingly meditative journey or an infinite roller-coaster ride through hell.

The ships are piloted out of the bay to the Beagle Channel. The channel is about 240km long and is about 5km wide at its narrowest point. From the channel, the ships enter Drake Passage,

**BELOW** The *Academic Ioffe* – floating home for runners and support personnel.

**RACE:** Antarctica Marathon
**LOCATION:** King George Island, Antarctica
**DISTANCE:** 42.2km (26.2 miles), single stage
**DATE:** February
**TOTAL ASCENT:** 680m (2,230ft)
**TOTAL DESCENT:** 680m (2,230ft)
**KEY CHARACTERISTICS:** Arrive by ship across Southern Ocean. All trail course with glacier ascent
**RACE RECORDS:** Male: 3:50, Female: 4:20 (unofficial – slight course changes each year)
**FIELD (APPROX):** Limited to 180
**CLIMATE:** -10° to 0°C (15°F to 32°F) less wind chill. High probability of rain, sleet or snow
**FINISHERS:** 90–95% of starters.
**RACE DIRECTOR:** Thom Gilligan
**EMAIL:** info@marathontours.com
**WEB:** www.marathontours.com

the 1,000km body of water between Cape Horn, Chile and the South Shetland Islands. This tumultuous mass of water forms part of the Southern Ocean and is the shortest crossing from Antarctica to the rest of the world. The passage's namesake was the 16th-century English explorer Sir Francis Drake.

The ships pass tremulously by Cape Horn, which is 146km south of Ushuaia. This is the most southern (and most feared) of the mariners' three great capes of the Southern Ocean. It marks the northern boundary of the Drake Passage and its surrounding waters are notoriously hazardous, due to strong winds, large waves, and icebergs.

*'I, the albatross that awaits for you at the end of the world…*

*I, the forgotten soul of the sailors lost, rounding Cape Horn from all the seas of the world.*

*But die they did not in the fierce winds, for today towards eternity, in my wings they soar, in the last crevice of the Antarctica winds.'*

SARA VIAL, *ALBATROSS MEMORIAL* AT CAPE HORN (1992)

**RIGHT** Small Zodiacs are used to ferry competitors to explore ice formations – and to the start line.

**ABOVE** Acclimatizing to the
environment amongst the locals.

## Arriving in Antarctica

Race founder and organizer, Thom Gilligan, says:

*'People will say that they had no interest in going somewhere like Antarctica until they heard there was a marathon there. But afterward, they are talking about the experience, not just the race. So you need to have a good race and a good destination to make it work.'*

The first days exploring in Antarctica are an assault on the senses for the Antarctic marathon participants. The all-consuming and overwhelming sensation of just being in that environment is extraordinarily difficult to capture in words. Jules Verne tried in *20000 Leagues Under the Sea*, describing it thus:

*'I cannot express my astonishment at the beauties of these new regions. The ice took most surprising forms. Here the grouping formed an oriental town, with innumerable mosques and minarets; there a fallen city thrown to the earth, as it were, by some convulsion of nature. The whole aspect was constantly changed by the oblique rays of the sun, or lost in the greyish fog amidst hurricanes of snow. Detonations and falls were heard on all sides, great overthrows of icebergs, which altered the whole landscape like a diorama.'*

Amidst this intriguingly mystical setting, competitors are able to explore the
tangle of bays in the Shetland Islands and Antarctica Peninsula. The ship itself,
built by the Russians for this very type of terrain, is surprisingly nimble as it ducks
in and out of bays and weaves through the headlands. When it reaches its limits,
out come the zippy little Zodiacs that stealthily manoeuvre in and out among the
icebergs and floes to ferry competitors to amazing seal and penguin colonies.

At Deception Island, the horseshoe-shaped flooded volcanic caldera,
competitors can enjoy a 'swim' in the thermal pools along the shoreline.
Passengers are also able to disembark to explore the aptly named, Paradise Bay.
There is a once-in-a-lifetime opportunity to camp at the bay, which is on the
Antarctic continent itself. Rarely does one get the opportunity to sleep on the 'Last
Continent', and it should not be passed over lightly, even if it does not create an
ideal pre-race conditioning environment.

## The Antarctic Marathon Race Day

As runners are just starting slowly to begin to comprehend this overwhelmingly new and alien environment, race day is suddenly upon them. The unshakeable sense of unease inevitably creeps back to take hold. It is one thing to explore the Antarctica in the relative safety of a Russian icebreaker or a professionally operated Zodiac, but to compete in that environment in the solitary sport of marathon running is something else. Gilligan summed it up when he said:

*'Antarctica just has this magic appeal because it's the most demanding race and the most remote location.'*

Nonetheless, by the time race day approaches, competitors have shared eight wonderful days of adventure and discovery. There is a sense of camaraderie among the participants. But Day Nine is the reason for the journey. And on Day Nine, everyone also becomes a competitor, pitched against one another and/or against the Antarctic itself.

The first challenge on race day is the mission to get ashore. By Day Nine at sea, competitors would have acquired some experience at disembarking using the small (and relatively flimsy) Zodiacs. The swell at King George Island can raise itself to a quite fearsome height. But after nine days at sea to get to the start line, it would take extraordinarily bad conditions to dissuade competitors from getting to the start line for the 9am starting gun (presumably not in breach of the Antarctica Treaty).

There are some grim tales in the history of the Antarctic Marathon, arising from the difficulty of getting runners to the start line. These have inevitably been woven into race legend. In 1997, only half of the competitors made it ashore in time for

**BELOW** The 'crux' of the figure-of-eight marathon course – two ascents of the Collins Glacier.

the official start. The rest were forced to watch from the boat as the field set off to the starter gun. Fortunately, they were able to land and start the race 2.5 hours later. In 2001, things were even worse when no runner was able to disembark due to the severe wind conditions. In a tale from 'Runners' Hell', competitors were forced to race 422 laps around the ship deck. In 2003, the full field did make it to the start line in time for the starter gun, but only after braving extremely high seas and, during the race, gale-force winds amid 1.8m snowdrifts.

Competitors are provided with race numbers and pins before disembarking, but are encouraged to wrap up warm for the shuttle to shore and change into race clothes inside the Russian base. Equipment is largely a matter of personal choice for this event. That said, fell or orienteering shoes are a real benefit to runners on the lethally slippery glacier section of the course. In terms of clothing, conditions are best suited to a thermal base layer with light windproof outer shell. A good hat, warm gloves and socks are essential. It can get very, very cold. Apart from the cold and the dryness, there are no particular conditions that necessitate any special type of race training – just basis marathon race fitness and some experience with off-road and undulating terrain.

Temperatures range from minus 10°C to 0°C (10°F–30°F). The wind chill can lower the temperature by another 10°C. Heavy snow is rare, but light flurries are common. Humidity is extraordinarily low, which makes conditions dry and harsh. These islands are considered to have the mildest living conditions in Antarctica, with an average winter temperature in August of -6.8°C, and +1.1°C in February (the warmest time of the year when the race is held).

It is important to be prepared for the worst. As the race organizer said in 2002, *'this is Antarctica, where adversity and unpredictability are the norm.'* He said of the 2002 event that *'Race conditions were ideal if you like high winds and snow gales.'*

The course itself is a standard marathon distance of 42.2km. It has never been AIMS certified due to its ever-changing glacial shifts and conditions.

The race route comprises a two-lap figure-of-eight beginning and ending at the Russian base, Bellingshausen Station. Bellingshausen was one of the first research stations founded by the Soviet Antarctic Programme in 1968. It has a summer population of 25 to 50 people (a few of whom come out to compete in the event). It passes from Bellingshausen through the Uruguayan (Artigas) and Chilean (Frei) bases to the southern tip of the figure-of-eight and the Chinese (Great Wall) base at the northern tip (with Bellingshausen at the central cross-over point).

The bases have an almost frontier-like atmosphere that plays its own part in the history and conduct of the race. In 1997, the second time the race was held, race officials bartered with members of the Russian base, exchanging a crate of fresh fruits and vegetables, a case of Stolichnaya vodka, 10 bed linens and teaspoons, in exchange for use of the facilities during the event. It was a worthwhile exchange – the base provides an indispensable shelter for runners to warm up and refuel while waiting to journey back to the ship.

The run is 'manned' at key points by hardy souls who brave the unforgiving wind and cold. However, there are no official drinks stations and competitors are required to bring three of their own 500-600ml (16 or 20oz) water bottles. These

**ABOVE** The final steps in 'The Last Marathon' – on the last continent.

are dropped at strategic points en route by race staff, to be collected by passing runners. It is a good idea to tape a sports bar or energy gel to the drink bottle: it helps identify it in the bottle mountain and gives an energy boost as well as something to look forward to.

Approximately 600m past the Uruguayan base is the foot of Collins Glacier, which is reached via a 4.8km dirt road from Bellingshausen. It is a 1.1km ascent up the glacier to a height of 150m. The surface is snowy and icy and perilously slippery. Going up is a challenge; coming down may be deadly.

Extreme conditions bring out superhuman performance and endurance. This event is no exception. In 2005, wheelchair athlete William Tan completed the Antarctic half-marathon in under six hours, using a modified racing chair that had to be equipped with studded snow tires and ice axes for the glacier.

After descending the glacier, competitors return along the road (up and down small, sharply undulating hills) back through the Uruguayan, Russian and Chilean bases. It is then a lonely 4.5km trek in the opposite direction up to the turnaround point at the Chinese base. This is sited at a remote and lonely point reminiscent of remote and isolated outposts at the far reaches of China's own Silk Road. From there, competitors make their way back to the Russian Base to start the second loop.

In addition to the occupants of the multi-national research bases, other spectators include a bevy of bird and marine life, among them chinstrap penguins and southern elephant seals.

# Post Race BBQ (and Kayak Championship)

The next day, as the ships cruise among the fjords and islands, race organizers host a fabulous barbecue prize-giving event on the rear deck. Each and every finisher receives a certificate and a (deservedly chunky) medallion hailing successful completion of 'The Last Marathon'.

In 1995, the inaugural Antarctica Marathon on 'The Last Continent' made it possible for runners to complete marathons on each one of world's seven continents, and to earn membership to the elite Seven Continents Club (SCC).

THE PART OF THE ANTARCTIC that provides the stage for the Antarctic Marathon is the South Shetland Islands. The rosary of islands, which were named after the Shetland Islands off the north coast of Scotland, consist of 11 major islands and several minor ones. Although the Islands are subject to sovereignty claims from the United Kingdom, Chile and Argentina, the Antarctic Treaty means that their sovereignty was frozen. Hence they are free for use by any signatory of the Treaty for non-military purposes.

King George (also known as Isla 25 de Mayo by Argentinians and Vaterlo (Waterloo to Russians) is the largest island in the Shetland Islands chain. It is over 90% glaciated and approximately 95km long and 25km wide. It is located about 120km off the coast of the Antarctica mainland. King George Island was discovered by the British explorer William Smith in 1819, who claimed the islands for King George III. In 1821, 11 men of the sealing vessel *Lord Melville* survived the Antarctic winter on the island (the first ever 'winter over').

King George Island now houses scientific research stations for nine separate sovereign states. These include Argentina, Brazil, Chile, China, South Korea, Peru, Poland, Russia, and Uruguay. There is one airfield, owned by Chile. And there is one Russian Orthodox wooden church, Trinity Church, near Russia's Bellingshausen Station.

The bizarre 'community' of King George Island epitomizes the unique political status of Antarctica. Nine sovereign nations peacefully co-exist. All operate within their own, separate area and cultural boundaries. They interact but do not integrate.

Competitors in the Antarctic Marathon have the surreal experience of running 42.2km through a piece of each of Argentina, Russia, Chile and China. In the course of the event, partipants are cheered on in at least four languages from countries that are usually separated by half a globe and a whole world of cultural difference.

Finally, in order to satisfy the remaining competitive appetite of the sportsmen and women on board, the race organizers host the finals of the Antarctica Kayaking Championship in the fjords near the Lemaire Channel. This is the stuff legends are made of.

## Homeward Bound

There are moments in the rolling journey down to Antarctica that participants find themselves wondering how they possibly will survive 10 days on board the icebreaker with its bobbing and swaying and its rudimentary facilities. But by the time the ship has turned its bow to leave the White Continent in its wake, one cannot help but feel a real tug of sadness. Ten days seem a flash that has passed by in a dream.

There is no doubt that the lives participants are heading back to will be greatly enriched for having made this extraordinary journey.

**ABOVE** Warming up for the finals of the Antarctica Kayaking Championship.

# ANTARCTIC ICE
# **MARATHON**

THE ANTARCTIC ICE MARATHON was originally conceived as the South Pole Marathon, a marathon ending at the magnetic South Pole at the centre of the Antarctic ice shelf. However, organizing a run to the South Pole proved to be difficult logistically and involved major expedition-style planning, preparation and expense. Consequently, organizers settled for the Antarctic Ice Marathon, which takes place at 80° South in the foothills of the Ellsworth Mountains – not quite the South Pole, but deep in the Antarctic interior nonetheless. As it is one the last remaining wildernesses in the world, the Antarctic interior rates as the most isolated location for a marathon.

**BELOW** Race headquarters – the Patriot Hills Base Camp near the Ellsworth Mountains.

The foothills of the Ellsworth Mountains are located at an altitude of 3,000m. Due to the thickness of the atmosphere over the pole, physiologically it is equivalent to an altitude of 3,700m. Conditions are harsh. The average annual rainfall is on a par with the Sahara desert. The air is dry and bitterly cold. Katabolic winds of up to 322km per hour tear across the plains of ice, which can be up to 3km thick.

Competitors in the Antarctic Ice Marathon are ferried by a large Russian aircraft from Punta Arenas, Chile, to the Patriot Hills Base Camp. The aircraft can land on the blue-ice runway only if there is good visibility, a well-defined horizon and the wind speed is less than 20 knots.

The Antarctic Ice Marathon course is a single 42km figure-of-eight loop across snow groomed by snow-mobile. It is nonetheless an uneven running surface. A continual light dusting of soft, drifting snow settles on the uneven terrain and creates the effect of running on sand. Competitors who choose to use snowshoes will need to trial these in training, as they create a different running gait. It is vital

**ABOVE** The lead bunch – demonstrating the importance of forward momentum.

'No person who has not spent a period of his life in those "stark and sullen solitudes that sentinel the Pole" will understand fully what trees and flowers, sun-flecked turf and running streams mean to the soul of a man.'
**Ernest Shackleton**

**RIGHT** Essential equipment while
running in Antarctic conditions –
a neoprene balaclava and ski
goggles.

**OPPOSITE** A worthy celebration
upon completing the unique
event.

to keep the peripherals warm (hands, feet, face) with appropriate layers of clothing, as these are the most vulnerable to cold-related conditions such as frost nip.

Small fluorescent markers indicate the edge of the track and large bamboo poles act as mile markers. Aid stations are placed 8–9km apart and the course is constantly patrolled by support staff on snow-mobiles. With such a small field, runners soon spread out and one of the biggest challenges is coping with the isolation in the vast, blindingly white expanse of snow.

Running in such an extreme environment presents many problems, but one of

## THE 100KM ULTRA OPTION:

AS IF THE MARATHON was not hard enough, there is also an option to run a 100km ultra race. Richard Donovan was the only runner for the first event, finishing in an incredible time of 15:43:15, paced only by his MP3 player.

But word spreads fast in the ultra-running community and by the second event, Richard was joined by 6 other hardy souls for an epic day on the ice. The spur of competition helped Richard to push the race record down to 12:55:06 but the last man was not home for another 10 hours. It is worth noting that 5 of the 7 runners had competed in the Marathon 2 days earlier!

the most unusual is dealing with bodily waste. The Antarctic is an extremely environmentally sensitive area and all manmade material bought into the camp must be returned to Chile; this includes human waste. Runners, therefore, must make appropriate provision and run with a spare bottle for fluid output.

The cost of the Antarctica Ice Marathon means that it will remain a niche event attracting elite, sponsored athletes or committed eccentrics. It is unlikely that the opportunity to race in the 'Last Desert' will fall into one's lap, but should fate deal the ace card, it is one opportunity not to be missed.

## KEY DATA

**RACE** Antarctic Ice Marathon

**LOCATION** Foothills of Ellsworth Mountains, Antarctica

**DISTANCES** 42.2 & 100km, single stages

**DATE** December

**TOTAL ASCENT** Negligible

**TOTAL DESCENT** Negligible

**KEY CHARACTERISTICS** Arrive by aircraft from Punta Arenas, Chile. Ice trail on Antarctic interior

**RACE RECORDS** Male: 5:08, Female 6:33 (42.2km)/ Male:12:55 (100km)

**FIELD (APPROX)** Limited to 25

**CLIMATE** -20°C (-4°F) to -10°C (14°F)

**FINISHERS** 100% of starters (since inception)

**RACE DIRECTOR** Richard Donovan

**EMAIL** rd@icemarathon.com

**WEB** www.icemarathon.com

# NORTH POLE
# **MARATHON**

THE CREATION of the North Pole Marathon gave adventure runners the opportunity to complete the 'Grand Slam' of extreme running: Seven Races on Seven Continents and the North Pole. This is unequivocally the northern-most marathon in the world.

In 2002, having just completed and won the first South Pole Marathon, Richard Donovan heard a rumour that runner-up Dean Karnazes was quietly planning a trip to the North Pole to become the first runner to complete a marathon at each pole. In the true spirit of polar adventure and international competition, Donovan tried to head the American off at the pass. As Karnazes made his way north through Canada, Donovan negotiated a passage with a Russian vessel through Norway. Karnazes never made it and Donovan completed his solo assault on the North Pole in just under four hours.

**BELOW** Race record holder Sean Burch, running strongly. Snow shoes are recommended to ensure reliable traction underfoot.

The Arctic is not the eighth continent, but rather a floating mass of ice. At its winter peak, the Arctic covers an area approaching that of the United States, receding markedly in the summer months. The permanently dark winters are characterized by clear skies and stable weather. Under the 24 hour summer sun, stormy weather is common and deposits of fresh snow are frequent. It is bitterly cold all year round. Even in the marginally warmer summer months, runners contend with temperatures as low as -30°C. Wind chill may drive temperatures down further to -40°C. Any exposed skin is prone to frost-nip, or worse, if not suitably protected.

The journey to the North Pole is as much an adventure as the race itself. The international field assembles at Longyearbyen, the principle town in the Norwegian islands of Svalbard. This is the most northerly town served by a scheduled airline. It is a frontier town, which was originally established to service the mining, hunting and fishing industries. More recently, it has become a base for tourism and the launch of polar expeditions.

After one final night of relative comfort, competitors are transported by specially adapted Anotonov cargo plane for the two-and-a-half hour flight to a Russian encampment, known incongruously as 'Ice Station Barneo'. The Russian aircraft itself is from another era, but is reliable and strong and able to cope with the harsh conditions. At camp Barneo, a 1km runway has been bulldozed out of the snow and is marked by lines of black, snow-filled bin-bags. Camp Barneo is re-established every summer to provide support to polar expeditions and scientific surveys in the area. For their short stay at the North Pole, competitors are accommodated in heated tents and dine communally. The constant daylight and extreme cold both have a considerable effect on the physical and psychological well-being of participants prior to the commencement of the event.

Following the inaugural event, race organizers decided not to attempt to run the race to the magnetic North Pole itself, but instead to run it in the vicinity of Camp Barneo. At the end of the day, any

## KEY DATA

RACE  North Pole Marathon
LOCATION  89N–90N, Arctic Ice Cap
DISTANCE  42km (26.2 miles), single stage
DATE  April
TOTAL ASCENT  Negligible
TOTAL DESCENT  Negligible
KEY CHARACTERISTICS  Coldest, most northerly marathon held on ocean pack ice
RACE RECORDS  Male 3:36, Female 5:52
FIELD (APPROX)  Limited to 24 from 2008
CLIMATE  -30°C (-22°F) less wind-chill
FINISHERS  100% of starters (since inception)
RACE DIRECTOR  Richard Donovan
EMAIL  rd@npmarathon.com
WEB  www.npmarathon.com

fixed point has little meaning on a constantly moving mass of ice and the race route would inevitably drift from its starting point in any event. Perhaps more significantly, as the field has grown in size, the additional facilities that Borneo provides are necessary for ensuring the safety of all competitors.

The average ice thickness of the Arctic is approximately 3m. Internal pressure forces it to buckle to form hillocks and small ice cliffs. In addition fissures, known as 'leads', cause breaks in the ice exposing the Arctic Ocean beneath, which serves as a sober reminder that this race is not taking place on land. The conditions underfoot vary considerably. Compacted snow creates a layer of hard ice, which is broken and uneven. Overlying the rough surface is a light covering of snow, which drifts in the strong Arctic winds and obscures the uneven surface.

Competitors need to ensure that they take great care to protect body extremities from the cold during the run. At least two pairs of thick socks are required with additional protection for the toes. To accommodate the bulk, competitors need running shoes that are a couple of sizes larger than normal.

'The North Pole Marathon is the most amazing extreme marathon I have ever run. It brought runners to the limits of their endurance and lived up to its billing in every respect, affording athletes a chance to run and feel on top of the world.'

**Michael Collins, Ireland (International Novelist and 2006 Winner)**

Many of the runners wear snow shoes to assist traction. Thermal and windproof layers are necessary to cover the legs and body, gloves and mittens for the hands, and neck scarves, a balaclava, a face mask and goggles for the head. The polar explorer look is thus complete. Race organizers provide a heated tent along the route to permit competitors to adjust layers or simply take shelter from the cold. It is within this refuge that the small support team play a vital role, melting snow to mix up isotonic drinks to fuel the freezing runners.

Running on top of the world, under the midnight sun, surrounded by the icy moonscape-like vista is a surreal experience. The relative ease of the journey to the North Pole serves to belie the unreal nature of this event. Perhaps this really is the last frontier in extreme running: afterall, once the Seven Continents have been conquered, all that is left is the North Pole Marathon.

**LEFT** 42.2km and once around the Pole.

# INDEX

# PICTURE ACKNOWLEDGEMENTS

BaikalExpress/www.baikal-marathon.de 116, 117; Nicola Bartesaghi 80; James Boka 137, 140, 141, 142, 146; Comrades Marathon Association 54, 55; Graham Dainty – New Zealand/www.photofiordland.co.nz 11, 118-119, 120, 121, 124, 125, 126, 127, 128 left & right, 129; GORE-TEX ™ Transalpine-Run by Plan B event company GmbH/Pictures by W. L. Gore & Associates 10, 14-15, 30, 31; Le Grand Raid de La Réunion/Noël Thomas 56, 57; Rob Howard 104, 106, 107, 108, 111, 112, 113 top & bottom; Jungle Marathon Ltd 84, 87, 89, 92, 93, 94, 95; Kappes Adventure Press 12, 81, 85, 88 bottom, 90, 91; Mike King/www.mikekingphoto.com 1, 2-3, 8, 9, 134-135, 148, 149, 150, 151, 152, 153, 154, 155; Chris Kostman 67, 72 right, 73, 74; John Lindsay 132, 133; Chris Lusher, Racing The Planet 82-83, 96, 100-101, 114, 115; Kym McConnell 26 top & bottom, 43 top & bottom, 63, 64, 65 top, 75 left, 88 top, 102, 136, 139, 143, 144-145, 147; David Nelson 60-61, 65 bottom, 66, 69, 71, 72 left, 75 right; For The North Face Ultra-Trail du Tour du Mont-Blanc ® /Cyril Bussat 19, 22, /Jean-Pierre Clatot 16, 18, 25, /Pascal Fayolle 23, /Flash Sport 24, 27, /Helen Le Bouchellec 21; Pikes Peak Marathon, Inc 76, 77; Bryce Quarrie 130, 131; Pierre-Emmanuel Rastoin/www.rastoin.com 6-7, 36-37, 38-39 top, 38 bottom, 40, 41, 44-45, 46-47, 48, 49, 50, 51 top & bottom, 52, 53 top & bottom; Dave Remington 62, 68; Michael A. Shoaf, Racing The Planet 4-5, 97; Spartathlon/Angelos Venetsianos 33, 34; Stephen Speckman 78, 79; Glenn Tachiyama 35; Trans 333/Alain Gestin/www.extreme-runner.com 58, 59; Verdon Canyon Challenge 'Ultrail'/Manu Maule 28, 29; Carl Yarbrough 98, 99.

Front cover: Pierre-Emmanuel Rastoin/www.rastoin.com
Back cover: Mike King/www.mikekingphoto.com

# ACKNOWLEDGEMENTS

FIRST AND FOREMOST we wish to acknowledge Kate Oldfield from Pavilion Books who agreed to meet for a coffee and discuss our proposal for a book centred on extreme running. From the outset Kate supported our concept and without her backing this book would never have been published – we sincerely thank her for her belief in us and the project.

We express our gratitude to Sir Ranulph Fiennes for kindly agreeing to write the Foreword for this book. He continues to be a true inspiration to us all.

## Race Directors

The authors would like to thank the following race directors and organizers for their support, encouragement and guidance in completing this book.

Catherine & Michel Poletti, Ultra-Trail du Tour du Mont-Blanc; Patrick Bauer, Marathon Des Sables, Atlantide Organisation Internationale; Chris Kostman, Badwater Ultramarathon, Adventure CORPS; Diana Penny Sherpani, Everest Marathon, Bufo Ventures Ltd; Shirley Thompson, Jungle Marathon, EventRate; Steve Norris, Kepler Challenge Organizing Committee; Thom Gilligan, Antarctica Marathon, Marathon Tours & Travel; Richard Donovan, North & South Pole Marathons, Polar Running Adventures; Jean Giacosa & Patrice Wasescha, Verdon Canyon Challenge; Uta Albrecht, Transalpine-Run; Panagiotis Tsiakiris, Spartathlon; Renee Smith & Katia Jones, Comrades Marathon; Robert Chicaud & Véronique Victorie, Le Grand Raid de la Réunion; Alain Gestin & Melinda Chantrel, Trans 333; Ron Ilgen & Matt Carpenter, Pikes Peak Marathon; John Grobben, Wasatch Front 100 Miler; Robert Pollhammer, Yukon Artic Ultra; Catherine Cole & Mary K. Gadams, Atacama Crossing & Gobi March, Racing The Planet; Andreas Kiefer & Alexei Nikiforov, Lake Baikal International Ice Marathon; Devy Reinstein, Inca Trail Marathon; Frances Piacun, Te Houtaewa Challenge; John Lindsay & Michael Grayling, Bogong to Hotham Trail Run; Diana Zadravec, Kepler Challenge; Patrice Malloy, Antarctica Marathon.

## Photographers

Many people kindly donated their race photographs to us. In addition, the following photographers made an exceptional contribution to the success of this project: Graham Dainty, Dave Remmington, Nicola Bartesaghi, Angelos Venetsianos, Stephen Speckman, Carl Yarbrough, Mike King, Dave Nelson, Rob Howard, Pierre Emmanuel Rastoin, Christiane Kappes, Alan Dunster, and Jim Boka.

## For Pavilion Books

We thank Anna Cheifetz for sponsoring this book; Kate Burkhalter for managing the project; Emma O'Neill for photography support, Vanessa Bird for creating the index; and Austin Taylor for his design work. We greatly appreciate the tireless efforts of Martin Darlison in creating the maps throughout the book.

## Personal Support

Kym wishes to thank his family for believing in his dreams and never questioning his plans, in particular Wendy, Samuel and Toby, collectively the best support crew anyone could wish for.

Dave would especially like to thank his family, Peter Burge, Jake & Diane Iles, Ian & Kate Tripp and Katrina Doherty for their unrelenting support throughout this venture.

In the course of running these races we have met numerous runners, support personnel and many other characters along the way. We thank you for assisting us on our journey and sharing many emotions.